Collins
English for Exams

Listening
for IELTS

Fiona Aish &
Jo Tomlinson

Collins

HarperCollins Publishers
The News Building
1 London Bridge Street
London
SE1 9GF

First edition 2011

10 9 8 7 6

© HarperCollins Publishers 2011

ISBN 978-0-00-742326-2

Collins ® is a registered trademark of HarperCollins Publishers Limited

www.collinselt.com

A catalogue record for this book is available from the British Library

Typeset in India by Aptara

Printed in China by RR Donnelley APS.

About the authors

Jo Tomlinson has a broad range of experience teaching academic English and IELTS in both private college and university settings, including online assessment.

Fiona Aish has managed and taught on various exam and academic English programmes at private language schools and universities, and has been preparing students for IELTS for over 10 years.

Jo and Fiona are co-owners of Target English, an English language training company that specialises in preparing and supporting university students in the UK. They are also the authors of *Grammar for IELTS* (Collins, 2012).

Authors' acknowledgements

The authors would like to thank their families, especially their parents, Peter and Sylvia Tomlinson and Brian and Linda Aish, for their continuing support. We would also like to thank Jim Leslie, Mike Burrows, Angela Must and Penny Leslie for their help and advice. And a final word of thanks goes to Howard Middle, Tasia Vassilatou and the team at HarperCollins.

Photo credits:

All images are from Shutterstock.

Cover: Edyta Pawlowska; p8: Anton Gvozdikov, Dmitrijs Dmitrijevs, CREATISTA, Phil Date, pzAxe, Deklofenak, StockLite, michaeljung; p16: Monkey Business Images; p17: Kuzma, absolute-india, Mihail Zhelezniak; p24: Martin Fischer, ronfromyork, Maridav, Tyler Boyes, kwest, B747; p32: Jaren Jai Wicklund, wavebreakmedia, Hurst Photo, CREATISTA; p34: Monkey Business Images, Goodluz; p38: Susan Law Cain; p40: chuckstock, Brocreative; p48: alersandr hunta, Tracy Whiteside, DanielW, Evgeniy Gorbunov, Picsfive, Mike Flippo; p56: WDG Photo; p64: gyn9037, Aaron Kohr; p72: dotshock; p88: JeremyRichards, Photobank.

Contents

Introduction

Who is this book for?

Listening for IELTS will prepare you for the IELTS Listening test whether you are taking the test for the first time, or re-sitting the test. It has been written for learners with band score 5-5.5 who are trying to achieve band score 6 or higher.

The structured approach, comprehensive answer key and model answers have been designed so that you can use the materials to study on your own. However, the book can also be used as a supplementary listening skills course for IELTS preparation classes. The book provides enough material for approximately 50 hours of classroom activity.

Content

Listening for IELTS is divided into 12 units. Each unit focuses on a topic area that you are likely to meet in the IELTS exam. This helps you to build up a bank of vocabulary and ideas related to a variety of the topics.

Units 1–11 cover the key types of questions that you find in the IELTS Listening test. Every exercise is relevant to the test. The aims listed at the start of each unit specify the key skills, techniques and language covered in the unit. You work towards Unit 12, which provides a final practice IELTS Listening test.

Additionally, the book provides examination strategies telling you what to expect and how best to succeed in the test. Exam information is presented in clear, easy-to-read chunks. 'Exam tips' in each unit highlight essential exam techniques and can be rapidly reviewed at a glance.

Unit structure

Each of the first 11 units is divided into 3 parts.

Part 1 introduces vocabulary related to the topic. A range of exercises gives you the opportunity to use the vocabulary – clearly and effectively – in a variety of contexts. These exercises also build awareness of the patterns in words and language items. The vocabulary is presented using Collins COBUILD dictionary definitions.

Part 2 provides step-by-step exercises and guidance on specific question types that appear in the test. Each unit covers one section from the test and focuses on three question types. There are explanations and examples that show you how to approach each question type. Useful tips are highlighted to help you develop successful test-taking strategies.

Part 3 provides exam practice questions for the same section of the test that you did exercises for in Part 2, using the same question types. The format follows the actual exam. You can use this as a way of assessing your readiness for the actual exam.

Answer key

A comprehensive answer key is provided for all sections of the book including notes on why certain answers are correct or incorrect. You will also find full audio scripts of all listening exercises at the back of the book. The answers are underlined in the audio scripts so you can see where the correct answers come in the audio.

Using the book for self-study

If you are new to IELTS, we recommend that you work systematically through the 12 units in order to benefit from its progressive structure. If you are a more experienced learner, you can use the aims listed at the start of each unit to select the most useful exercises.

Each unit contains between three and four hours of study material. Having access to someone who can provide informed feedback on the listening practice exercises is an advantage. However, you can still learn a lot working alone or with a study partner willing to give and receive peer feedback.

Ideally, you should begin each unit by working through the **Part 1** vocabulary exercises. Try to answer the questions without looking at a dictionary in order to develop the skill of inferring the meaning of unfamiliar words from context. This is important because dictionaries cannot be used during the actual exam. Avoid writing the answers to vocabulary exercises directly into the book so that you can try the exercises again once you have completed the unit.

Work through the **Part 2** listening exercises from beginning to end. It is important to study the notes about each of the question types so that you become familiar with how to approach the different question types in the test. Doing this will also help you develop more general skills for listening. The strategies covered should be thoroughly mastered so that during the actual exam you are fully prepared for each section and can focus on 'listening'. All learners, including those who are working on their own, should attempt the listening tasks as listening is a skill that can only be improved through extensive practice. At the same time, you should aim to become well-informed about a wide variety of subjects, not just those covered in the book. The IELTS Listening test can cover almost any topic considered to be within the grasp of a well-educated person. Listening regularly to English language news programmes and lectures can help with this, too.

Part 3 contains exam practice questions. After you have done the test, it is a good idea to spend some time reviewing why certain answers are the correct ones. For this reason we suggest you approach this part in the following way.

First do the test. Here, you focus on answering the questions correctly. You should try and complete Part 3 within the time limit set and listen only once, as this gives you the opportunity to practise under exam conditions. Do not look at the audio script at the back of the book while doing the test. After you have finished listening, make sure the format and spelling of your answers is correct. Then, check your answers using the Answer key.

Then learn from the test. Here, you focus on understanding why certain answers are the correct answers. When you have checked your answers, you can listen again to try to hear any answers that you missed. Reading the audio script at the same time as listening to the recording will help you to develop your listening skills and identify answers. Remember that the answers are underlined in the audio scripts.

Unit 12 is a complete practice listening test. This unit should be done under exam conditions. You should answer all four sections consecutively and listen only once. Please also take into account the timings for the breaks within the sections. Normally, in the actual test you would keep 10 minutes aside to transfer your answers. Please bear this in mind when doing Unit 12.

The International English Language Testing System (IELTS) Test

IELTS is jointly managed by the British Council, Cambridge ESOL Examinations and IDP Education, Australia.

There are two versions of the test:

- Academic
- General Training

Academic is for students wishing to study at undergraduate or postgraduate levels in an English-medium environment.

General Training is for people who wish to migrate to an English-speaking country.

This book is primarily for students taking the Academic version.

The Test

There are four modules:

Listening	30 minutes, plus 10 minutes for transferring answers to the answer sheet NB: the audio is heard *only once*. Approx. 10 questions per section Section 1: two speakers discuss a social situation Section 2: one speaker talks about a non-academic topic Section 3: up to four speakers discuss an educational project Section 4: one speaker gives a talk of general academic interest
Reading	60 minutes 3 texts, taken from authentic sources, on general, academic topics. They may contain diagrams, charts, etc. 40 questions: may include multiple choice, sentence completion, completing a diagram, graph or chart, choosing headings, yes/no, true/false questions, classification and matching exercises.
Writing	Task 1: 20 minutes: description of a table, chart, graph or diagram (150 words minimum) Task 2: 40 minutes: an essay in response to an argument or problem (250 words minimum)
Speaking	11–14 minutes A three-part face-to-face oral interview with an examiner. The interview is recorded. Part 1: introductions and general questions (4–5 mins) Part 2: individual long turn (3–4 mins) – the candidate is given a task, has one minute to prepare, then talks for 1–2 minutes, with some questions from the examiner. Part 3: two-way discussion (4–5 mins): the examiner asks further questions on the topic from Part 2, and gives the candidate the opportunity to discuss more abstract issues or ideas.
Timetabling	Listening, Reading and Writing must be taken on the same day, and in the order listed above. Speaking can be taken up to 7 days before or after the other modules.
Scoring	Each section is given a band score. The average of the four scores produces the Overall Band Score. You do not pass or fail IELTS; you receive a score.

IELTS and the Common European Framework of Reference

The CEFR shows the level of the learner and is used for many English as a Foreign Language examinations. The table below shows the approximate CEFR level and the equivalent IELTS Overall Band Score:

CEFR description	CEFR code	IELTS Band Score
Proficient user (Advanced)	C2 C1	9 7–8
Independent user (Intermediate – Upper Intermediate)	B2 B1	5–6.5 4–5

This table contains the general descriptors for the band scores 1–9:

IELTS Band Scores		
9	Expert user	Has fully operational command of the language: appropriate, accurate and fluent with complete understanding.
8	Very good user	Has fully operational command of the language, with only occasional unsystematic inaccuracies and inappropriacies. Misunderstandings may occur in unfamiliar situations. Handles complex detailed argumentation well.
7	Good user	Has operational command of the language, though with occasional inaccuracies, inappropriacies and misunderstandings in some situations. Generally handles complex language well and understands detailed reasoning.
6	Competent user	Has generally effective command of the language despite some inaccuracies, inappropriacies and misunderstandings. Can use and understand fairly complex language, particularly in familiar situations.
5	Modest user	Has partial command of the language, coping with overall meaning in most situations, though is likely to make many mistakes. Should be able to handle basic communication in own field.
4	Limited user	Basic competence is limited to familiar situations. Has frequent problems in understanding and expression. Is not able to use complex language.
3	Extremely limited user	Conveys and understands only general meaning in very familiar situations. Frequent breakdowns in communication occur.
2	Intermittent user	No real communication is possible except for the most basic information using isolated words or short formulae in familiar situations and to meet immediate needs. Has great difficulty understanding spoken and written English.
1	Non user	Essentially has no ability to use the language beyond possibly a few isolated words.
0	Did not attempt the test	No assessable information provided.

Marking

The Listening and Reading papers have 40 items, each worth one mark if correctly answered. Here are some examples of how marks are translated into band scores:

Listening: 16 out of 40 correct answers: band score 5
                    23 out of 40 correct answers: band score 6
                    30 out of 40 correct answers: band score 7

Reading   15 out of 40 correct answers: band score 5
                    23 out of 40 correct answers: band score 6
                    30 out of 40 correct answers: band score 7

Writing and Speaking are marked according to performance descriptors.
Writing: examiners award a band score for each of four areas with equal weighting:

- Task achievement (Task 1)
- Task response (Task 2)
- Coherence and cohesion
- Lexical resource and grammatical range and accuracy

Speaking: examiners award a band score for each of four areas with equal weighting:

- Fluency and coherence
- Lexical resource
- Grammatical range
- Accuracy and pronunciation

For full details of how the examination is scored and marked, go to: www.ielts.org

1 On the move

Part 1: Vocabulary

1 Match the words a–h to the pictures 1–8.

a	customers ___	**c**	staff ___	**e**	tour guide ___	**g**	travel agent ___
b	passenger ___	**d**	receptionist ___	**f**	tourist ___	**h**	waiter ___

2 Learning words related to a topic is a good way to increase your vocabulary for the IELTS Listening exam. Complete the passage about hotels below with the words a–h. There are two possible answers for four of the gaps.

a	alternative	**c**	old-fashioned	**e**	sufficient	**g**	traditional
b	common	**d**	reasonable	**f**	suitable	**h**	unique

> The Grand Hotel was built in 1900 and has a(n) (1) _____ style; there is nothing like it in the local area. Although the interior design is (2) _____, the facilities are modern. The hotel has a conference centre and meeting rooms so it is (3) _____ for business purposes.

A(n) (4) _____ option is the Hotel Royal, which is a(n) (5) _____ choice for tourists because the prices are (6) _____, and it is next to the beach. The hotel is not modern; in fact it is quite (7) _____ and in need of minor repair, but it is (8) _____ for a short break.

3   Match the words 1–8 with their synonyms a–h.

1 suitable _____	a conventional
2 traditional _____	b frequent
3 alternative _____	c dated
4 unique _____	d other
5 old-fashioned _____	e adequate
6 reasonable _____	f appropriate
7 sufficient _____	g fair
8 common _____	h individual

4   Choose the sentence which does **not** mean the same as the key sentence.

1   The price of dinner was reasonable.

   a   I thought the meal was a fair price.
   b   The bill for dinner was not too expensive.
   c   That meal was overpriced.

2   Three hours will be sufficient to see all of the art gallery.

   a   Three hours should give you enough time to see everything in the art gallery.
   b   I think three hours is an adequate amount of time for viewing the art gallery.
   c   You'll be unlikely to see all the art gallery in three hours.

3   I don't think this hotel is suitable for children.

   a   This hotel is quite satisfactory for families.
   b   I wouldn't recommend bringing under 18s to this hotel.
   c   This hotel isn't appropriate for minors, in my view.

4   Heavy rain is common in this area at this time of year.

   a   There is often bad weather here at this time of year.
   b   At this time of year there are occasional storms around here.
   c   In this region rain is frequent at this time of year.

Part 2:   Practice exercises

1

01 CD1

You are going to listen to two university students discussing their holiday plans. Look at the listening task below and predict the kinds of answers you are listening for.

Listen and write the missing information. Write NO MORE THAN THREE WORDS AND/OR A NUMBER for each answer.

Jenny's holiday plans		
	Predictions	**Answer**
Destination:	1 _Place_	4 _Mexico_
Length of holiday:	2 _weeks_	5 _6 weeks_
Type of holiday:	3 _beach_	6 _Interrailing_

Now check your answers.

2

01 CD1

Read the sentences 1–6 below and predict the answers based on the content and grammar of each sentence.

Listen to the same conversation as you heard in Exercise 1 and complete the sentences.

Steve's holiday plans	
Predictions	**Answers**
1 Steve is going on holiday for _____.	4 Steve is going on holiday for _Paris_.
2 He is going on holiday with his _friend_.	5 He is going on holiday with his _friend_.
3 He is going on holiday in order _____ French.	6 He is going on holiday in order _study_ French.

Now check your answers.

> ⓘ **Exam information: Form completion (1)**
>
> In the IELTS Listening exam, you may have to complete a form. This question type can often be found in Section 1. Normally, each answer is one or two words. In Section 1, the information is factual; for example, dates, places and times.

3 Look at the form below. If this were an exam task, what kind of information would you be listening for (place, time, name, date)?

OUTBOUND FLIGHT DETAILS	
Full name:	1 _____
Telephone number:	07953 299101
Flight number:	JK402
Depart:	London Heathrow
Arrive:	2 _____
Departure time:	3 _____
Date of travel:	4 _____

4 The information needed to complete a form can be expressed in different ways. Look at the examples 1–7 below and write *name*, *date*, or *time* next to each one.

1 Mr R. D. Davison _____

2 Ten fifteen _____

3 Ronald Davison ... D–A–V–I–S–O–N (spelling) _____

4 July twenty-third _____

5 A quarter past ten _____

6 Davison .... Ronald Davison _____

7 The twenty-third of July _____

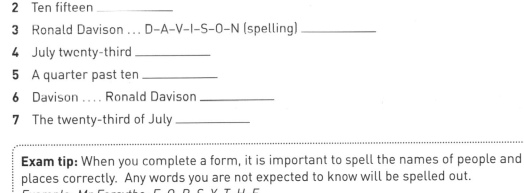

> **Exam tip:** When you complete a form, it is important to spell the names of people and places correctly. Any words you are not expected to know will be spelled out.
> *Example: Mr Forsythe: F–O–R–S–Y–T–H–E*
>
> Words you are expected to know will not be spelled out.
> *Example: 23 North Street*

🎧 **5** **02 CD1**

Complete the form below. Write **NO MORE THAN THREE WORDS AND/OR A NUMBER** for each answer.

ROOM BOOKING	
Name:	**1** Duncan _____
Telephone number:	5762 23821
Date of arrival:	**2** _____
Date of departure:	23rd September
Room type:	Twin room
Cost:	**3** £ _____
Payment method:	**4** _____

Exam tip: In the IELTS Listening exam, it is very unusual for the words you read to be the words you hear on the recording. You should listen for different ways of expressing the same idea.

Now check your answers.

ⓘ **Exam information: Matching (1)**

In the IELTS Listening exam, you may have to match pieces of information. Such tasks can be found in any section of the exam.

6 Look at the listening task below. If this were an exam task, you would have to match the tour operators with the type of service they offer. Match the sentences 1–6 that describe a service with the services a–d in the listening task.

1 The service is fast. _____

2 If you have your student card, there is a cheaper rate. _____

3 This has the lowest prices. _____

4 It is only £3.50, which is the least expensive ticket. _____

5 The service isn't very regular. _____

6 There is 10% off for students. _____

Tour Operator	Service
1 Stanford Coaches	a offers the cheapest fare
2 ABSEL Buses	b has an infrequent service
3 Grey Bus Company	c runs an express bus
4 Flyers Coach Company	d has a student discount

7 Listen to the conversation between a customer and a travel agent. Match the hotels to the facilities they offer. Write a–d next to questions 1–4.

1	Hotel Sunshine _____	a	fitness facilities
2	The Highland Hotel _____	b	business facilities
3	Hotel Carminia _____	c	training courses for water sports
4	The Royal _____	d	entertainment facilities

03 CD1

> ℹ **Exam information: Multiple choice (1)**
>
> In the IELTS Listening exam, there are different types of multiple-choice questions. The first type has a number of questions, each of which has three answer options. You have to choose the answer option which is correct according to the recording. This is called a multiple-choice single-answer question.

8 Look at the multiple-choice single-answer question below and three ways of expressing the same question.

Why can't John go on the boat trip? = *Why isn't it possible for John to go on the cruise? – Why can't John go sailing? = Why isn't it possible for John to take part in the boat trip?*

    a He doesn't feel well.
    b He has booked theatre tickets.
    c He is scared of the water.

Think of two other ways of expressing each answer option a–c.

9 Listen and choose the correct answer.

04 CD1

  1 Why can't John go on the boat trip?

    a He doesn't feel well.
    b He has booked theatre tickets.
    c He's scared of the water.

10 Listen and answer the questions about John and Sam's holiday.

05 CD1

  1 Where does Sam recommend going for dinner?

    a Joe's Café
    b The Captain's Table
    c Mangan's

  2 Who is going to reserve the table?

    a John
    b Sam
    c The hotel receptionist

Part 3: Exam practice

Exam tip: Don't always write down the first thing you hear. The recording often refers to a number of possible answers, but only one answers the question correctly. Look at this example conversation between a tourist and a travel agent about the date of a flight:

Tourist: I'd like to fly out on the twenty-third of July ... that's the Sunday, isn't it?
Travel agent: No, that's the Saturday ... the twenty-fourth is the Sunday ...
Tourist: Then the twenty-fourth ... Yes, I'd like to go on the Sunday.

The answer would be July 24th, **not** July 23rd.

SECTION 1
QUESTIONS 1–4

06
CD1

Complete the form below.

Write **NO MORE THAN TWO WORDS AND/OR A NUMBER** for each answer.

City Bus Tour Booking Form	
Number of passengers:	2
Passenger name(s):	Susan Field and James **1** _____
Contact telephone number:	07988 **2** _____
Hotel:	**3** _____
Bus tour time:	**4** _____ p.m.
Bus tour date:	14th August

QUESTIONS 5–6

07
CD1

Choose the correct letter **A**, **B** or **C**.

5 Why does a ticket for the museum cost £10?

   A The money is needed to fix parts of the building.

   B The collection of Latin American art is unique.

   C It is the only art museum in Europe.

6 The tourist office assistant suggests going to the next town for a good restaurant because

   A they overlook the sea.

   B the restaurants are bigger.

   C there are more restaurants to choose from.

QUESTIONS 7–10

🎧
07
CD1

Match the restaurants with their descriptions.

Write **ONE** letter **A–E** next to questions 7–10.

7	The Belleview	_____
8	The Lighthouse Café	_____
9	Harvey's	_____
10	Stonecroft House	_____

A   It is visited by famous people who work in entertainment.

B   This restaurant has recently been bought by a new family.

C   One family has managed the restaurant for over 100 years.

D   It is expensive but serves high quality food.

E   It has been decorated in a modern style.

2 Being young

Aims: Following instructions | Using the correct format | Building words
Completing tables | Labelling maps or plans | Completing flow charts

Part 1: Vocabulary

1 Match the pictures 1–3 above with the words a–e. More than one option may be possible.

a a child ___   **c** a baby ___   **e** a toddler ___

b an infant ___   **d** an adolescent _3_

2 Match the words 1–5 with the definitions a–e.

1 youth _a_	a the period between childhood and maturity
2 youth hostel ___	b a place that provides leisure activities for young people
3 youth club ___	c inexpensive accommodation for young people travelling cheaply
4 youth culture ___	d a person between the ages of thirteen and nineteen
5 teen/teenager ___	e distinct styles, behaviours, and interests characterised as being of and from young people

3 Understanding word formation is very important, as your answers will need to be grammatically correct. Complete the table with the correct word forms. The first one is done for you.

Verb	Noun	Adjective	Adverb
act	action/activity	active	actively
motivate	1 _____	2 _____	–
3 _____	4 _____	practiced/practising	–
5 _____	6 _____	7 _____	successfully
8 _____	instruction	9 _____	10 _____
concentrate	11 _____	12 _____	–
–	13 _____	capable	14 _____
15 _____	16 _____	expressive	17 _____

4 Complete the sentences 1–4 with the correct word form of *act*.

1 I'm a very _____ person.

2 I always _____ quickly in emergencies.

3 I do lots of different _____ in my spare time.

4 I always participate _____ in class.

5 Read what the young people below do outside school and complete the texts with the correct word form of the words in the box. You will need to use some words twice.

act   concentrate   instruct   practise   motivate   succeed

James: At the moment I'm studying for my exams, so I'm not very (1) _____. I haven't played any sports for ages! I'm trying to (2) _____ on my revision as I want to pass all my exams. I do have guitar lessons every Thursday, though, which I really enjoy. My (3) _____ is fantastic, and he encourages me. I really should (4) _____ more, though!

Helen: I love playing sports, and I go to hockey (5) _____ three times a week. I know that's quite a lot, but I'd like to play hockey professionally, and this goal (6) _____ me to work hard. I also play tennis and football, and I go swimming twice a week. I have an annual membership to the local sports centre as I'm there every day!

Mike: I really love computers and spend a lot of my time creating computer games for fun. Lots of people say computer games are a bad thing, but I think these games take a lot of (7) _____; you need to keep your mind on the game at all times. I suppose sitting in front of a computer is not the most (8) _____ of hobbies, but I'd like to be a(n) (9) _____ designer of computer games one day.

Part 2: Practice exercises

1   Look at the table below which shows the exam results of two students. Choose the correct options a–h to complete the table.

Exam results

Student name	Subject	Score
Brian Andrews	1 _____	67.5%
2 _____	English	3 _____%

a	french	**c**	Charlotte	**e**	Charlotte Black	**g**	56.7%
b	French	**d**	C Black	**f**	fifty-six point seven	**h**	56.7

ℹ **Exam information: Table completion (1)**

In the IELTS Listening exam, you may have to complete a table. This question type can be found in any section of the exam.

You have to complete the table with words or options from a list.

🎧 08 CD1

2   Listen and complete the following table. Write NO MORE THAN TWO WORDS AND/OR A NUMBER for each answer.

Shimmers Dance Classes Timetable

Class	Instructor	Day	Time	Price
Ballet	1 _____	Tuesday	6.30–8.00	2 £ _____
3 _____	Janine	4 _____	7.00–8.00	£7.50
Tap	Andrew	Saturday	5 8.30–_____	£11.00

3 Answers can be more difficult than names and numbers. You are going to hear a talk about websites for young people. Listen and complete the table. Write NO MORE THAN TWO WORDS AND/OR A NUMBER for each answer.

09
CD1

Website	Age range	Useful for:
Playtime Online	4–6	Learning skills for games
Moving Up	1 _____	Developing maths and language skills
Net Aware	12–16	Understanding 2 _____
Chat Electric	13–16	Making 3 _____
4 _____	16–18	Exam hints and tips

> ### *i* Exam information: Labelling a map or plan (1)
>
> In the IELTS Listening exam, you may have to label a map or plan. This question type can be found in any section of the exam.
>
> There will be some visual information (a map or plan) which you have to label by writing the information yourself or choosing the answer from a list of options. The information you need in order to answer the questions is in the same order as it is on the recording.

4 Look at the plan of a summer camp in Exercise 5. Match the phrases a–f with the places on the map 1–3. You will need to use each number twice.

a right next to the washrooms
b beside the river
c at the riverfront

d the furthest away from the river
e in the centre of the camp
f right in the middle of everything

5 Listen and label the plan below. Write NO MORE THAN THREE WORDS AND/OR A NUMBER for each answer.

10
CD1

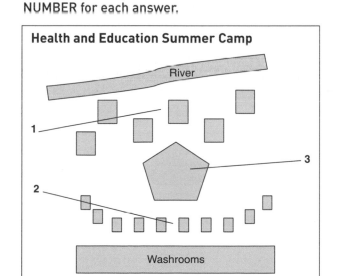

Health and Education Summer Camp

River

Washrooms

1 _____
2 _____
3 _____ area

> **ℹ** **Exam information: Flow chart completion (1)**
>
> In the IELTS Listening exam, you may have to complete a flow chart. A flow chart is a diagram that shows the order in which things happen, or a process. Each box usually shows a separate stage in the order or process. The boxes are normally separated by a line or arrow, which shows the flow or order. This question type can be found in any section of the exam.
>
> You have to complete the flow chart by writing up to three words and/or a number, or choosing the answer from a list of options.

6   Look at the flow charts A and B below and read the information in Texts 1 and 2. Match A and B with 1 and 2.

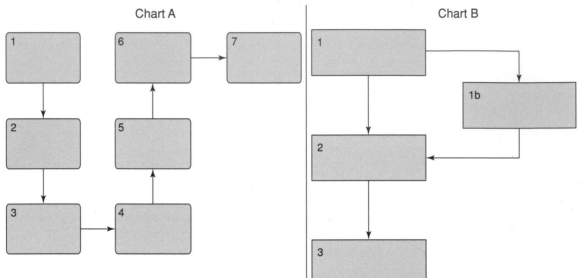

Chart A

Chart B

Text 1
If you want to come on this French exchange trip then you will need to complete the admission form. If you aren't a member of the French exchange club, you will need to become a member of the club at the same time as completing the admission form. After you have completed the form you will need to pay the visit deposit. This is £45. After you have done this, we will send you a letter confirming your place.

Text 2
To enter the five-a-side football tournament, you firstly need to make sure you have a team of seven (five to play and two substitutes) and then elect a captain for your team. Fill in an application from the sports club and list your team name, members and captain on the form. Then, pay the £10 entrance fee. We will then send you the times and dates you will play at. When you receive these, you will need to call and confirm with our club secretary that you can attend all the dates. Once you have done this, we will also send you an invitation to the tournament opening event, which will take place in our club house the evening before the first match.

Chart: _B_

Chart: _A_

7 Write the correct information from the Texts 1 and 2 in Exercise 6 in the flow charts. Use the number of boxes and the lines or arrows to help you. For this exercise ONLY you may write as many words as you like.

8 You are going to hear a talk about completing the Duke of Edinburgh's Award. Listen and complete the flow chart below. Write NO MORE THAN THREE WORDS AND/OR A NUMBER for each answer.

11
CD1

Getting the Bronze Award

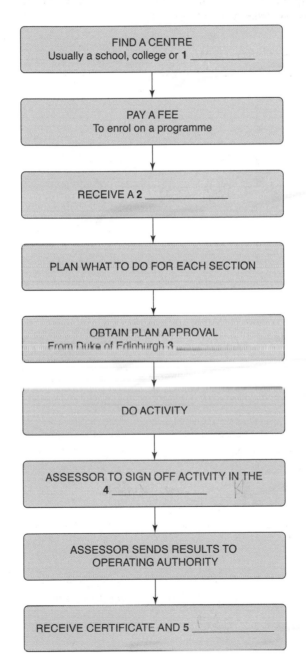

FIND A CENTRE
Usually a school, college or **1** _____

PAY A FEE
To enrol on a programme

RECEIVE A **2** _____

PLAN WHAT TO DO FOR EACH SECTION

OBTAIN PLAN APPROVAL
From Duke of Edinburgh **3** _____

DO ACTIVITY

ASSESSOR TO SIGN OFF ACTIVITY IN THE
4 _____

ASSESSOR SENDS RESULTS TO
OPERATING AUTHORITY

RECEIVE CERTIFICATE AND **5** _____

SECTION 2
QUESTIONS 1–4

🎧
12
CD1

Complete the table below.

Write **NO MORE THAN TWO WORDS AND/OR A NUMBER** for each answer.

Park Hill Teen Programme

Class	Day	Teacher
Jazz	Wednesday	Diana
1 _____	Thursday	Diana
Baseball	Saturday	2 _____
3 _____	Sunday	Steve
Skateboarding	Monday	Steve
4 _____	Tuesday (to be confirmed)	Stella

QUESTIONS 5–7

🎧
13
CD1

Label the plan below.

Write **NO MORE THAN TWO WORDS AND/OR A NUMBER** for each answer.

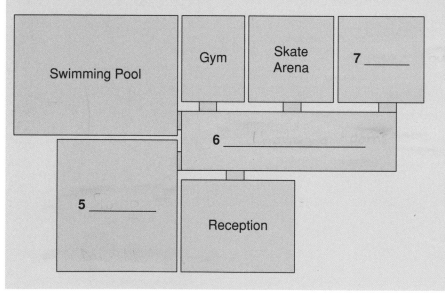

QUESTIONS 8–10

Complete the flow chart below.

Write **NO MORE THAN TWO WORDS AND/OR A NUMBER** for each answer.

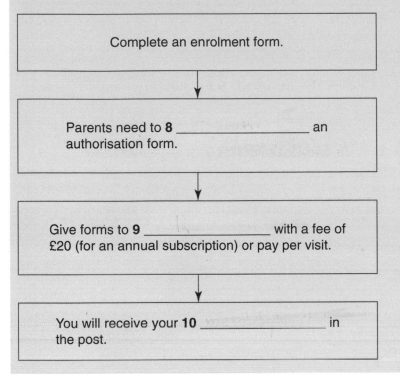

3 Climate

Aims: Spelling words correctly | Understanding the sequence of events
Following a conversation | Labelling a diagram | Completing notes
Classifying

Part 1: Vocabulary

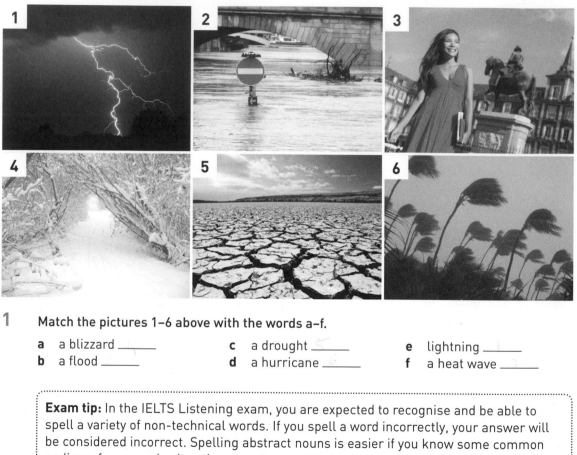

1 Match the pictures 1–6 above with the words a–f.

a	a blizzard _____	**c**	a drought _____	**e**	lightning _____
b	a flood _____	**d**	a hurricane _____	**f**	a heat wave _____

Exam tip: In the IELTS Listening exam, you are expected to recognise and be able to spell a variety of non-technical words. If you spell a word incorrectly, your answer will be considered incorrect. Spelling abstract nouns is easier if you know some common endings, for example *-ity, -tion, -ment, -ness*.

2 Listen and write the words 1–9. First you will hear the word and then you will hear the word in a sentence.

CD1
14

1 _____   4 _____   7 _____

2 _____   5 _____   8 _____

3 _____   6 _____   9 _____

3 Complete the sentences 1–8 with the words a–h to form common weather collocations. You can use one word more than once.

a clear   c heavy   e light   g strong
b flash   d high   f scorching   h thick

1 There is a chance of _____ / _____ rain in the morning, so take an umbrella with you.

2 There are _____ winds on the coast, so be very careful if walking near the cliffs.

3 There have been _____ floods in the south of the country and many people have had to evacuate their homes at short notice.

4 The north has been affected by _____ snow, and many people are snowed in at home.

5 Today will be sunny with _____ blue skies.

6 There is _____ fog in the west and driving might be dangerous.

7 There will be _____ temperatures in the afternoon today, so make sure you drink plenty of water.

8 We advise people not to take their children out in the _____ heat.

4 Underline the odd one out in the groups of words 1–4 below and say why it is different.

Example: cool / hot / warm / balmy / rainy

'Rainy' is different: it does not describe temperature.

1 precipitation / moisture / humidity / atmosphere _____

2 global warming / climate change / greenhouse effect / ozone layer _____

3 tidal wave / hurricane / cyclone / gale _____

4 fog / haze / mist / drizzle _____

5 In the IELTS Listening exam you need to understand the sequence (or order) of ideas and/or events. Draw a table like the one below and put the sequencing words and phrases in the correct group. Some can go into more than one group.

during   initially   simultaneously
eventually   moving on to   the next phase/step
finally   next   ultimately
former   previously   when
in the end   prior

Before	After	At the same time	Transition from one stage to another

6 Complete the passage with the words a–h.

a during
b initially
c then
d prior

e simultaneously
f the next step
g ultimately
h when

Preparing for a Heat Wave

Make sure you are always prepared for any kind of extreme weather (1) _____ to it occurring. You can do this by checking the weather forecast regularly. Heat waves can often be predicted days and even weeks in advance. Heat waves are (2) _____ seen as fun, a chance to get outside in the sun, and a hazard, which can cause illness. Make sure you drink plenty of water (3) _____ this time, otherwise you may become dehydrated. (4) _____ you feel hot, try to find some shade.

It is also important to watch for signs of heatstroke. A person may (5) _____ become slow and lethargic, and (6) _____ become confused or incoherent. If you see these second symptoms, get the person into the shade immediately and give them water. If the symptoms do not go away instantly, (7) _____ would be to call an ambulance. If left untreated, heatstroke can (8) _____ lead to death.

7 Underline the correct words in the sentences 1–6.

1 Many people do not believe that pollution has disastrous long term effects on the environment, but *eventually / finally* they will have to accept the overwhelming evidence.

2 There was no *former / prior* warning of the storm; it took everyone in the village by surprise.

3 I was the only person standing under the large tree *during / when* the rain came so I was lucky and didn't get wet.

4 Here is the weather forecast for today. *Initially / Previously* it will be sunny, but cloud will develop later in the afternoon.

5 If a hurricane strikes, the first thing to do is get inside. *Next / The next step* you should shut all the windows and doors.

6 The effects of global warming will be seen in the future, *eventually / ultimately* leading to a dramatic rise in sea levels and *eventually / ultimately* flooding vast areas of low lying land.

Part 2: Practice exercises

🎧 1
15
CD1

In Section 3 of the IELTS Listening exam, you will hear up to four speakers and it is important to recognise the speakers.

You are going to hear a conversation with four speakers: John, Steven, Linda and Joanne. Listen and write how many times you hear each speaker. Two have been done for you.

John *3*   Linda *2*

Steven ___   Joanne ___

> **ⓘ Exam information: Classification (1)**
>
> In the IELTS Listening exam, you may have to decide which category or group items belong to. The categories are usually lettered (A, B, C, etc.) and the items are numbered (1, 2, 3). Your answer is usually a letter.

2   **Match the places 1–6 with the categories a, b or c.**

a Continent		1 Paris	_____
		2 Asia	_____
b Country		3 Brazil	_____
		4 Europe	_____
		5 Vietnam	_____
c City		6 Tokyo	_____

> **Exam tip:** Before you listen, think how the categories and items might be related, and try to think of other words that express these categories and items. One group, either the items or the categories, will probably be paraphrased.

🎧 3
16
CD1

You are going to hear a group of students talking about their Natural Earth presentation. Listen and match the tasks 1–5 with the person who will do them (a–c).

Natural Earth presentation: Who is doing which tasks?

a Alice		1 organise the research	_____
		2 make the PowerPoint presentation	_____
b Karl		3 source cloud images	_____
		4 write cue cards	_____
c Jenny		5 present the conclusion	_____

4   Look at the diagram which shows how acid rain is formed. Use the clues in the diagram and put the events a–d in the order they occur.

a   The wind carries the mixture of pollutants high into the atmosphere.

b   These fall in wet and dry forms.

c   Polluting emissions from cities enter the atmosphere.

d   The wet form runs into rivers, causing more pollution.

_____ _____ _____ _____

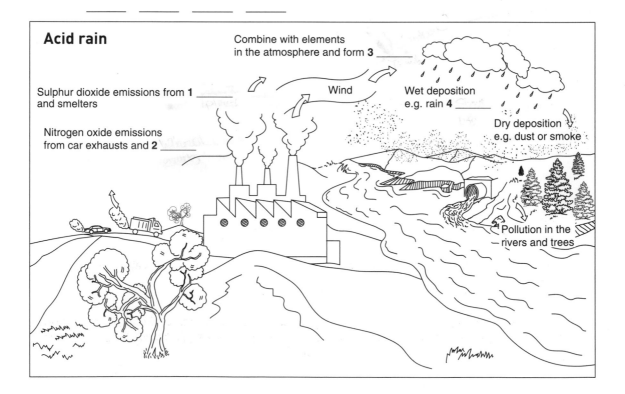

Acid rain

Combine with elements in the atmosphere and form **3** _____

Sulphur dioxide emissions from **1** _____ and smelters

Nitrogen oxide emissions from car exhausts and **2** _____

Wind

Wet deposition e.g. rain **4** _____

Dry deposition e.g. dust or smoke

Pollution in the rivers and trees

> **Exam tip:** If you have to label a diagram, always write the words you hear on the recording; do not use your own words.

5 You are going to hear two students discussing an assignment. Listen and complete the diagram in Exercise 4. Write NO MORE THAN THREE WORDS AND/OR A NUMBER for each answer.

17
CD1

> ℹ️ **Exam information: Note completion (1)**
>
> In the IELTS Listening exam, you may have to complete notes. This question type can be found in any section of the exam. You will need to think about the topic and look at the notes carefully to decide what kind of word fits grammatically in each space.

6 Read the notes and write what kind of word completes each space grammatically: a noun, a verb or a quantity/amount?

Lightning Safety: Presentation Plan

Part 1: Planning for lightning

- Important to be prepared
- Go inside before it **1** _____

Part 2: If inside

- Stay away from water, doors, windows, and telephones
- Turn off **2** _____

Part 3: If outside

- Avoid trees, open spaces, and metal objects
- If the lightning comes near you, **3** _____ and cover your ears

Part 4: If someone gets hit

- Get help from a **4** _____
- Call an ambulance
- Don't worry: **5** _____ of lightning victims survive!

Think of words related to the topic of 'lightning and safety' that could complete the notes above.

7 You are going to hear two students talking about a project. Listen and complete the notes in Exercise 6 above. Write NO MORE THAN THREE WORDS AND/OR A NUMBER for each answer.

18
CD1

SECTION 3
QUESTIONS 1–3

19
CD1

Complete the notes below.

Write **NO MORE THAN THREE WORDS AND/OR A NUMBER** for each answer.

Project suggestions: pros and cons
Localised weather conditions
Problem: Not enough time for **1** _____
Seasons
Problem: Too **2** _____
Extreme weather conditions
Advantage: Easier to **3** _____ into different sections, more interesting

QUESTIONS 4–7

19
CD1

Who will cover the following weather conditions?

A	Alex
B	Emma
C	Tom
D	None of them

Write the correct letter, **A**, **B**, **C** or **D** next to questions 4–7.

4 blizzards _____

5 floods _____

6 drought _____

7 cyclones _____

QUESTIONS 8–10

Complete the diagram below. Write **NO MORE THAN THREE WORDS AND/OR A NUMBER** for each answer.

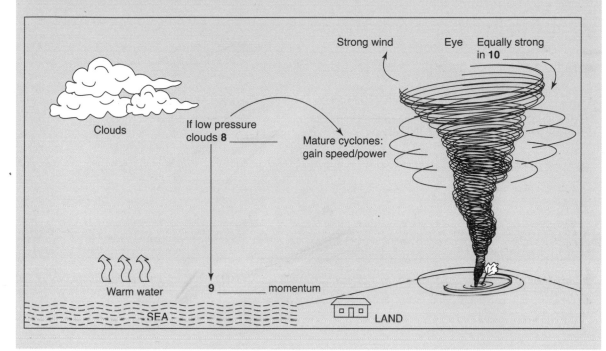

Strong wind   Eye   Equally strong in **10** _____

Clouds

If low pressure clouds **8** _____

Mature cyclones: gain speed/power

Warm water

9 _____ momentum

SEA

LAND

4 Family structures

Aims: Signposting and structuring | Using dependent prepositions
Answering short questions | Completing sentences/summaries
Selecting from a list

Part 1: Vocabulary

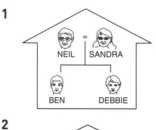

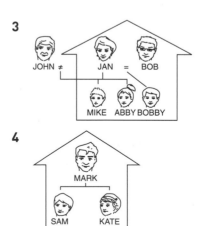

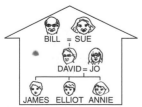

1   Match the words a–d with the family trees 1–4 below.

a   an extended family ____
b   a step-family ____
c   a nuclear family ____
d   a one-parent family ____

1
NEIL = SANDRA
BEN   DEBBIE

2
BILL = SUE
DAVID = JO
JAMES ELLIOT ANNIE

3
JOHN ≠ JAN = BOB
MIKE ABBY BOBBY

4
MARK
SAM   KATE

2   Read 1–8 and complete the words.

1 a member of your family	r_ _at_ _ _ (n)
2 to legally become husband and wife in a special ceremony	m_ _ _y (v)
3 a father or mother	p_ _ _nt (n)
4 money or property which you receive from someone who has died	in_ _ _ _ _an_ _ (n)
5 all the people in a family or group who live together in a house	h_ _ _ _h_ _d (n)
6 when two people are this, they have agreed to marry each other	e_ _a_ed (adj)
7 take someone else's child into your own family and make him/her legally your son or daughter	a_ _pt (v)
8 the child of your uncle or aunt	c_ _s_ _ (n)

3   Match the verbs 1–10 with the prepositions a–j that usually follow them.

1 participate _____	a with (person) about (thing)	**Exam tip:** In the IELTS Listening exam, your answers will need to be grammatically correct. It is important to read the questions carefully and decide what kind of word is missing. For example, some words must be followed by specific prepositions, and knowing which these are will help you write a grammatically correct answer. When you learn new verbs, make sure you know if they have a dependent preposition. A good dictionary will usually tell you this.
2 struggle _____	b with	
3 disapprove _____	c from	
4 concentrate _____	d of	
5 succeed _____	e in	
6 care (look after) _____	f at	
7 refer _____	g to	
8 suffer _____	h on	
9 agree _____	i in	
10 aim _____	j for	

4   Complete the sentences 1–8 with verbs and prepositions from Exercise 3. You may need to change the verb form.

1   Family members don't always _____ each other. In fact, they often argue!

2   Marion _____ her elderly mother, who is very frail.

3   Some people _____ unmarried couples living together; they think it's wrong.

4   The government plans are _____ helping poor families.

5   Young mothers often _____ looking after their newborn babies; the first couple of months can be very difficult.

6   Children should _____ many physical activities when they are young to keep them fit and healthy and help them socialise.

7   Parents can _____ many government websites for information about family support.

8   Today, some mothers are the main earners in families while the father stays at home and _____ raising the children as his main responsibility.

5 Here are two people talking about their families. Guess the missing words 1–9. They are all from Exercises 1–4.

Jenny

My family isn't very big. There's just my son and me. I'm a single (1) _____. For the last ten years I've been (2) _____ on looking after my son James, who is now fourteen. But now I've met someone special and we've just got (3) _____! My fiancé has four kids of his own and we're going to get married in July. James is really excited about it; he's looking forward to having brothers and sisters in his new (4) _____ family!

Sheila

We live as one big (5) _____ family. There are seven of us in our (6) _____. Besides my husband and me and our children, there's my aunt and two of my (7) _____. I stay at home and (8) care _____ my mother because she's quite old and can't look after herself. Obviously, we (9) _____ from a lack of space in the house, but we all get on well.

Now listen and check your answers.

21
CD1

Part 2: Practice exercises

> **Exam tip:** In Section 4 of the IELTS Listening exam, you will hear an academic lecture. When you listen to a lecture, it is important to be able to identify the key points and understand which direction it is taking. You can do this by identifying signposting words and phrases. For example, the function of 'but' is to introduce contrasting information.

1 What is the function of the signposting words in italics in the sentences 1–8?

a to give further information	**e** to indicate order
b to contrast	**f** to give a reason/reasons
c to emphasise	**g** to repeat or clarify
d to give an example/examples	**h** to indicate a result/results

1 *Firstly*, I am going to talk about the role of the parent. *Secondly*, ..., and *lastly*, ... _____

2 Parenting is a difficult job *because* ... _____

3 Families are important because they form the basis for socialisation. *Additionally*, ... _____

4 The family structure has varied greatly over time. *That is*, ... _____

5 Many argue that less traditional structures are not as effective. *However*, ... _____

6 Many people are having families later in life. *Consequently*, ... _____

7 Families in other parts of the world differ from the western norm. *For instance*, ... _____

8 Although there are many arguments for trying to keep the traditional family structure strong, I feel *the key issue is* ... _____

🎧 22
CD1

Now listen to how the sentences end and how they fulfil the functions a–h.

2 Draw a table like the one below and put the signposting words and phrases in the correct category according to their function.

a case in point is	for example	next
also	for instance	on the other hand
the reason for this is	furthermore	the crucial factor is
an illustration of this is	however	the main point is
as a result	in addition	thus
due to	in other words	what I am essentially
firstly	lastly	arguing is

Order	Reason	Result	Repetition/Clarification

Contrast	Addition	Example	Emphasis

3   Match the question words 1–8 and the type of answer a–h that each requires.

1 Where?	a a reason
2 Who?	b a place
3 When?	c a number
4 Why?	d a thing
5 What?	e a method/way
6 How?	f a person
7 Which?	g a thing (choice)
8 How many?	h a time

> **Exam tip:** In short-answer questions, it is important to be sure what the question is asking. One way to help you focus is to underline the key words before listening. Do not look only at the question words; the words in the rest of the sentence are also important. For example:
> *What reasons did he give for his choice?* = *Why did he choose it?*

4   Read the questions 1–4 and underline the key words. The first one is done for you. Then match the questions to the answers a–j. There is more than one correct answer for each question. Assign all letters a–j to one question.

1   On <u>average</u>, <u>when</u> do people get <u>married</u>? _____

2   What is the key reason given for the increase in divorce numbers? _____

3   Who believe that families are the key to the functioning of wider society? _____

4   What is the average number of family members in the UK? _____

a	People usually get married in their thirties.	**f**	Sociologists believe families are the key to the functioning of wider society.
b	The average family has five members.	**g**	5
c	Sociologists	**h**	Because there was a change in the law.
d	Legal changes	**i**	Because of legal changes.
e	In their thirties	**j**	Five

5 You are going to hear a lecture about adults who continue to live with their parents. Before listening, underline the question words and the key words in the questions 1–4. The first one is done for you.

1 <u>What percentage</u> of <u>women</u> in their early <u>thirties</u> still <u>live with</u> their <u>parents</u>?

2 When were house prices only three times the average yearly income?

3 What is the reason that people return to their parental home after university?

4 Who does the Affordable Housing Scheme aim to help?

🎧 **23**
CD1

Now listen and answer the questions in NO MORE THAN THREE WORDS AND/OR A NUMBER.

ⓘ **Exam information: Sentence and summary completion (1)**

In the IELTS Listening exam, you may have to complete sentences or a summary. This question type can be found in any section of the exam.

You have to complete the sentences or summary by writing the information yourself or choosing the answer from a list of options. The missing words must fit the space grammatically.

6 You are going to hear a lecture about family structures. What kind of information is needed to complete the sentences 1–4?

Example: Nowadays, the elderly are less likely to rely + `on + noun`.

- 'on': The verb 'rely' is usually followed by the dependent preposition 'on'.

- a noun: This sentence has a subject and a verb. To complete the sentence we need an object. This needs to be a noun because the verb 'rely on' is followed by an object. There may be a possessive adjective in front of the noun (e.g. '<u>their</u> siblings'), or an article (e.g. '<u>the</u> government').

1 The _____ family structure has changed greatly in the last fifty years.

2 Strong family structures used to be necessary due _____.

3 People often _____ the wealth of their parents.

4 More than _____ children have no siblings nowadays.

🎧 **24**
CD1

Now listen and complete the sentences using NO MORE THAN THREE WORDS AND/OR A NUMBER.

ⓘ **Exam information: Choosing answers from a list (1)**

In the IELTS Listening exam, you may have to answer a question by choosing a number of correct answers from a list. This question type can be found in any section of the exam.

You have to write the correct letters (A, B, C, etc.) and you may write these in any order.

7 Look at the photo and question below. Then underline the key words in sentences 1–5.

Which of the following are myths about upper-class Victorian* families?

1 Families lived with servants.

2 Children were mainly home schooled.

3 Fathers occasionally taught their children Latin.

4 The Victorians were not generous to the poor.

5 Parents were strict with their children.

*The Victorians were the British people who lived in the time of Queen Victoria, i.e. 1838–1901.

8 In the IELTS Listening exam, you probably will not hear the same words on the recording. You will hear paraphrases or synonyms.

Complete the sentences 1–5 with the words a–f so that they have the same meanings as the sentences in Exercise 7. The sentences are not in the same order.

a	resided	c	taught	e	hard
b	given	d	fortunate	f	give

1 Children were often _____ at home.

2 The servants _____ in the family home.

3 Mothers and fathers were _____ on their children.

4 The children were _____ lessons in Latin by their fathers.

5 These families didn't _____ to those less _____ than themselves.

9 You are going to hear a lecturer describing life for Victorian families. Listen and choose
25 TWO letters (a–e) to answer the question.
CD1

Which of the following are myths about upper-class Victorian families?

a Families lived with servants.

b Children were mainly home schooled.

c Fathers occasionally taught their children Latin.

d The Victorians were not generous to the poor.

e Parents were strict with their children.

Part 3: Exam practice

SECTION 4
QUESTIONS 1–4

Complete the sentences below.

Write **NO MORE THAN THREE WORDS AND/OR A NUMBER** for each answer.

1   Recent changes in society are eroding the traditional _____ structure.

2   Slightly fewer than 50% of American children under 13 live in _____.

3   Statistics show that cohabiting couples are more liable _____ than married couples.

4   DINKS focus on _____ rather than having children.

QUESTIONS 5–8

Answer the questions below.

Write **NO MORE THAN THREE WORDS AND/OR A NUMBER** for each answer.

5   How many children in the UK now live in single parent families? _____

6   According to some sociologists, who are responsible for the rise in single parenting?
_____

7   What have the largest group of lone parents never done? _____

8   Where are single parent families more likely to live? _____

QUESTIONS 9–10

Choose **TWO** letters, **A–E**.

Which two points does the lecturer give as disadvantages for living alone?

A   People living alone will need help from the community.

B   It is more likely to foster a fragmented population.

C   It creates an accommodation shortage.

D   It is more expensive for an individual to live alone.

E   People may have children too late.

9   _____

10 _____

5 Starting university

Part 1: Vocabulary

1   Underline the word that does not belong in each group 1–4 and decide why it does not belong.

    1 teacher, lecturer, student, tutor
    2 essay, report, presentation, dissertation
    3 book, journal, newspaper, brochure
    4 lecture, seminar, tutorial, lesson

2   Complete the passage with the correct form of words from Exercise 1.

The university is situated in the city centre and includes the faculties of Science, Engineering, Humanities, and Art. Each faculty has three subdivisions. Teaching is in the form of lectures, seminars and (1) _____, with the addition of labs and practical workshops for science and engineering courses. Each (2) _____ has a personal tutor, but other staff such as (3) _____ take some of the classes too. Assessment is through a variety of written work such as essays as well as oral (4) _____.

3 Learning which suffixes are used with verbs, nouns, and adjectives is a useful way to improve your grammatical accuracy in the IELTS Listening exam. Complete the table with the correct word forms.

Noun (subject)	Noun (person)	Adjective	Adverb
1 _____	astronomer	astronomical	astronomically
philosophy	philosopher	philosophical	2 _____
sociology	sociologist	3 _____	sociologically
statistics	4 _____	statistical	statistically
5 _____	politician	political	politically
biology	6 _____	biological	biologically
economics	economist	7 _____	economically
physics	8 _____	physical	physically

4 Complete the sentences 1–5 with the correct form of words from Exercise 3.

1 I find it so frustrating that _____ never give a straight answer when they are being interviewed on television. After all, we voted for them and they should be answerable to us.

2 I don't want to go out with John again. He's always asking _____ questions and making me think about the meaning of life. I would rather just talk about what happened during the day.

3 While _____ can be useful, people can always manipulate numbers to suit their needs.

4 _____ is the study of the nature of matter and energy.

5 I bought my friend a new telescope for her birthday. She loves looking at the stars; she's an amateur _____.

5 What word types end with the suffixes 1–8? Write *N* (noun), *NP* (noun person), *A* (adjective) or *AD* (adverb).

1 -ity _____   **3** -ally _____   **5** -ful _____   **7** -or _____

2 -able _____   **4** -ian _____   **6** -ment _____   **8** -ic _____

6 Complete the passage with the correct form of the words in brackets.

My name is Donald, and I'm a research student at Glasgow University. I work in the Biochemistry department and I'm researching how to make suntan cream from pure plant products. I find my work (1) _____ (*enjoy*) and fulfilling. At first I found it difficult to work alone, but now it's much easier. My (2) _____ (*supervise*) has been really (3) _____ (*help*) and she's shown me how to manage my time (4) _____ (*effect*) so that my daily workload is (5) _____ (*manage*). After I've completed this project, I'd like to continue doing (6) _____ (*science*) research.

Exam tip: When you learn new vocabulary, try to learn all the forms. For example: *nation (noun), national (adjective), nationally (adverb), nationalist (person), nationalise (verb)*

Part 2: Practice exercises

1   You are going to hear a student talking on the phone to her father about her university course. Before you listen, complete the sentences 1–4 in as many ways as you can.

    1   Sally likes her maths course because it is _____.

    2   She has four tutors who are _____, but she prefers Professor Jones due to his style of teaching.

    3   Although the course includes a lot of group work, Sally prefers to study _____.

    4   Sally is worried that she will _____ her statistics module as she finds it much harder than the others.

2   Listen and complete the sentences 1–4 above. Write **NO MORE THAN THREE WORDS AND/OR A NUMBER.**

27
CD1

> **ⓘ**   **Exam information: Labelling a map or plan (2)**
>
> In the IELTS Listening exam, the maps and plans are usually very simple, with some parts labelled. You should use the labelled parts as a guide when listening.

3   Listen and match the pictures 1–5 with the sentences you hear a–e. Write the letters a–e next to the question numbers 1–5.

28
CD1

1 _____		2 _____
Bank	Cinema	Supermarket / Bank / Cinema

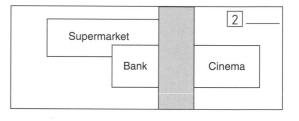

3 _____		4 _____
Bank / Supermarket	Cinema	Supermarket / Cinema / Bank

5 _____	Supermarket
Bank	

Exam tip: If you have to label a map or plan, think of ways you can describe where places are before you listen. You will need to think of vocabulary for directions, for example; *on the left, first right, along the road* and vocabulary for place or position, such as *opposite, next to, behind, at the end of the street.*

4   To complete a map, you need to be able to follow directions. Look at the map and complete the directions a–e with the numbers 1–5 on the map.

a   To get to _____ you need to go along the road from the supermarket.

b   Turn right out of the supermarket and take the first right. _____ is at the end of the road.

c   Walk over the bridge and just keep going straight along the road and you'll find _____.

d   Go left out of the Post Office and take the first left. _____ is on your right.

e   Go over the bridge and make a left turn. Then take the first right. _____ is on the left hand side of the street.

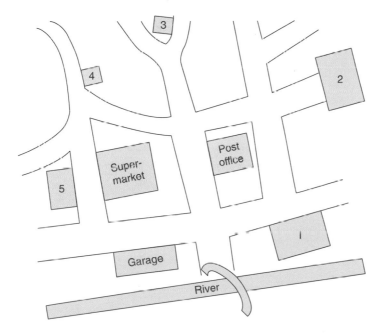

5   Look at the map again. You are going to hear two young people discussing what there is for university students to do in their town. Listen and write the names of the places 1–5 from the map in Exercise 4. You will not hear the same directions that were used in Exercise 4.

1 _____   4 _____

2 _____   5 _____

3 _____

🎧 **6**

30
CD1

Listen for the pauses in the addresses 1–3. The pauses show where the information is separated. Mark the pauses with commas on the addresses below.

1   78A High Trees Street Sydney 2316

2   354 Castle Avenue Edinburgh E5 7HU

3   86 The Drive New York 45008

🎧 **7**

31
CD1

You are going to hear a conversation between a student who is enrolling at university and a university administrator. Listen and complete the form below. Write **NO MORE THAN THREE WORDS AND/OR A NUMBER.**

Enrolment form

Name: Peter **1** _____

Course: BSc Economics

Faculty: **2** _____

University address: Room 112, **3** _____ Residence, Duke Street, Newcastle

Home address: 56, Grove Street, Manchester, **4** _____

---

8 Complete the notes with the information in the sentences a–d. Write NO MORE THAN TWO WORDS AND/OR A NUMBER.

a Students may borrow up to eight books from the library at any one time.

b The lecture on molecular biology has moved from room 102 to room 105.

c There are a limited number of university tours taking place this week so make sure you book your place as soon as possible to avoid disappointment. You can book in person through the Students' Union office or by telephoning Student Services.

d Feedback on your essay will be given by your personal tutor during the tutorial times. If you cannot attend the tutorial time, please speak to the administrator in the faculty office to arrange a more convenient time.

- Library book limit: **1** _____
- Room change for **2** _____ : Lecture room 105
- University tour booking procedures: Call Students' Services or book at Students' Union office **3** _____
- Essay feedback from: **4** _____ .

32
CD1

9 You are going to hear a student asking questions about the Students' Union services. Listen and complete the notes. Write NO MORE THAN TWO WORDS AND/OR A NUMBER.

Students' Union services

3 main areas:

- Give advice and information
- Organise **1** _____ events
- Campaign for students' rights

6 advisors: specialists in **2** _____ and travel

Location of 24-hour helpline number: **3** _____

SECTION 1
QUESTIONS 1–4

33
CD1

Complete the form below.

Write **NO MORE THAN THREE WORDS AND/OR A NUMBER** for each answer.

Name	Simon *Example: Anderson*
Student ID number	1 _____
Subject	Geography
Faculty	2 _____
Address	Flat 3, 24 **3** _____ Gardens, London, SW12 3AG
Contact telephone	07988 **4** _____

QUESTIONS 5–7

34
CD1

Label the plan below.

Write **NO MORE THAN THREE WORDS AND/OR A NUMBER** for each answer.

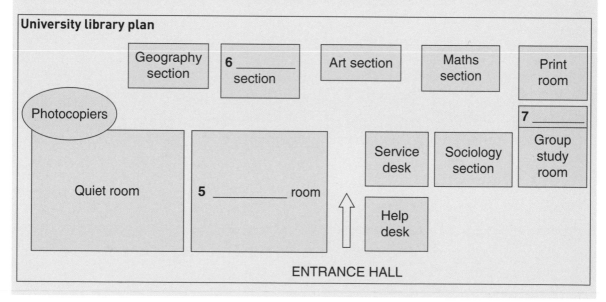

46   **Listening for IELTS**

QUESTIONS 8–10

34
CD1

Complete the notes below.

Write **NO MORE THAN THREE WORDS AND/OR A NUMBER** for each answer.

Group Study booking system

To be used for group projects

Advance notice required: 48 hours

Must reserve using **8** _____

Website booking for group study room – need student name and
9 _____

Booking confirmation received via **10** _____

---

6 Fame

Aims: Recognising paraphrases | Matching sentence fragments
Recognising distractors | Answering multiple-choice questions
Choosing answers from a list

Part 1: Vocabulary

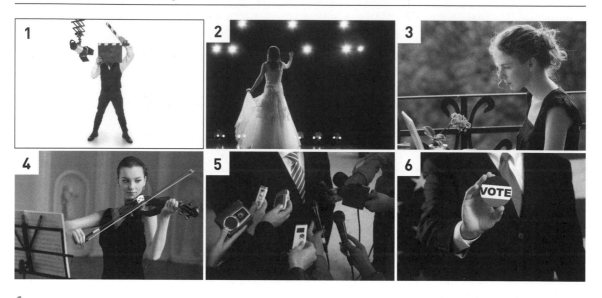

1 Match the pictures 1–6 above with the jobs a–f.

a actress ____   c director ____   e politician ____
b agent ____   d musician ____   f writer ____

2 Here are some people talking about their jobs. Underline the correct words in italics.
Sometimes both words are correct.

Hi, my name is Karl Harrison and I'm a writer. I've written for lots of films and some
television (1) *programmes / shows,* too. I only write (2) *scripts / plays;* I've never written
for the theatre. One day I would like to, I think. The best thing about my job is that it's
(3) *flexible / inflexible*: I can write whenever I want. And of course, I can be really
(4) *creation / creative*.

I'm Katie Cane and I am the (5) *star / fame* of the new Hollywood blockbuster *Reef*. I
love (6) *acting / playing*, but I always get followed everywhere by the (7) *press / media*,
which isn't so much fun. In *Reef*, I (8) *play / act* an Australian woman who's wanted by
the police. I love this (9) *character / personality*; she has a lot of depth.

I'm Edward Williams and I'm a film director. I've worked on many (10) *international /
national* projects around the world. My latest movie, *No More Limits*, was (11) *shot /
filmed* on (12) *location / site* in Japan. One of the best things about the job is that I
get to travel, and I can work with people from different countries. Film-making is
really my passion. I love films; my life without them would be (13) *unimaginable /
unintelligible*. I especially like the (14) *post-production / after-production* process, when
I can see the film finally taking shape.

3 A prefix is a letter or group of letters, for example 'un-' or 'multi-', which is added to the
beginning of a word in order to form a different word. Look at the words from Exercise 2
above:

- *inter + national – international* = across two or more nations
- *post- + production – post-production* = after production

Complete the table by adding the correct prefix, *bi, multi, re, pre, semi-* or *counter-* to the
words. The first one has been done for you.

Word	Word + prefix	Meaning of prefix
view	1 *preview*	before
productive	2 _____	opposite/opposite way
final	3 _____	half
national	4 _____	many
create	5 _____	again
lingual	6	two

4 Some words are made negative by using a prefix, for example:

- *un + imaginable – unimaginable* = not imaginable
- *in + flexible – inflexible* = not flexible

Complete the table by adding the correct prefix, *un, im, dis, in, ir* to the words.

Word	Word + prefix
equality	1 _____
trust	2 _____
perfect	3 _____
responsible	4 _____
aware	5 _____

5 Complete the words 1–6 in the passage with the correct prefixes.

I love being a musician because I get to use my creativity and talent. The only problem
is that the work is so (1) ____regular; I never know when I'm going to get paid. I'd love
to make a (2) ____-million-pound deal with a record label, but that's (3) ____likely to
happen. I like to dream, though! I played a few concerts last month, but if work doesn't
start coming in soon, I'm going to have to (4) ____-think my options. Some people think
I'm (5) ____responsible, but I just want to do the thing I love. Is that (6) ____reasonable?

Part 2:   Practice exercises

1   **If you paraphrase someone's words, you express what they have said or written in a different way. For example:**

The new action film is being released on Sunday. → The new action movie is coming out on Sunday.

Both these sentences have the same meaning, but some of the words are different.

Changing the word form and substituting synonyms are two common ways of paraphrasing. Look at the following examples:

- Substituting synonyms:

  *Helen Davies is the most **famous** person in this town. → Helen Davies is the most **well-known** person in this town.*

- Changing word forms:

  *Andrew Johnson **replaced** Jack Sullivan as the hero. → Andrew Johnson was Jack Sullivan's **replacement** as the hero.*

Paraphrase the sentences 1–4 by changing word forms.

1   Johanne De Vrie was the composer of 'Jules' Theme'.

Johanne De Vrie _____ 'Jules' Theme'.

2   Thomas Howard is recognised by the nation as the best president the country has ever had.

Thomas Howard is _____ recognised as the best president the country has ever had.

3   She performed really well in the new play.

She gave an excellent _____ in the new play.

4   The actor and director had creative differences.

The actor and director differed _____ .

Now paraphrase the sentences 5–8 by substituting synonyms.

5   It's the final night of the show.

It's the _____ night of the show.

6   Nicole was nervous because it was the premier of her film.

Nicole was nervous because it was the _____ of her film.

7   The prize for Best Score goes to Harriet James for the theme song 'Leaving Mississippi'.

The _____ for Best Score goes to Harriet James for the theme song 'Leaving Mississippi'.

8   The lead actor was fired from the film because of his bad behaviour.

The lead actor was _____ from the film because of his bad behaviour.

ⓘ Exam information: Matching (2)

In the IELTS Listening exam, you may have to match sentence beginnings with sentence endings. The words you read will not be the same as the ones you hear, so be prepared to listen for synonyms or paraphrases.

Look at the example below: the names 1–4 will not change, but the phrases/answers a, b, c, d will change:

1 Anna Collins
2 James Harman   WILL NOT CHANGE
3 Ian Cheriton
4 Sylvia Daniels

a has had ten bestselling books.
b was inspired by Tanbridge.   WILL CHANGE
c had a job in Tanbridge.
d is buried in the town.

---

2 The sentence endings i–vii are paraphrases of the sentence endings a–d. Some paraphrases involve changing word forms and some involve substituting synonyms. Match each sentence ending a–c with two sentence endings i–vii. Sentence ending d has only one paraphrase. The first one has been done for you.

	Changing word form	Substituting synonyms
a ... has had <u>ten bestselling books.</u>	*iii*	1 _____
b ... <u>was inspired</u> by Tanbridge.	2 _____	3 _____
c ... <u>is buried</u> in the <u>town.</u>	4 _____	5 _____
d ... <u>had a job</u> in Tanbridge.	–	6 _____

i ... drew on Tanbridge for many of his novels.

ii ... was laid to rest in Tanbridge.

iii *... has written many books, ten of which were bestsellers.*

iv ...'s burial took place here in Tanbridge.

v ... was employed in Tanbridge for many years.

vi ... found Tanbridge an inspiration for his novels.

vii ... had ten books which achieved massive sales.

🎧 **3**
35
CD1

You are going to hear a recording of a guide talking about the town of Tanbridge. Listen and match the people 1–4 with the sentence endings a–d.

1 Anna Collins _____
2 James Harman _____
3 Ian Cheriton _____
4 Sylvia Daniels _____

a has had ten bestselling books.
b was inspired by Tanbridge.
c had a job in Tanbridge.
d is buried in the town.

4 Read the sentence beginning and the three answer options below.

The Final Chapter is based on

a the director's travels in South America.
b a story the director heard.
c a novel.

In this type of multiple-choice question, there are three possible sentences, only one of which is correct:

- *The Final Chapter* is based on the director's travels in South America.
- *The Final Chapter* is based on a story the director heard in Mexico.
- *The Final Chapter* is based on a South American novel.

Now read the extract from the recording for the question above and identify the paraphrased sections. Then decide which answer option a–c is correct and why.

The Final Chapter is a murder mystery film set in South America. Written and directed by Bruce Chambers, it is a project very close to his heart. Chambers found inspiration for the film whilst travelling around South America. There he heard about a Peruvian book which tells the story of the fight for gold in South America. Reading this story, he at once realised this was a film he had to make.

> **Exam tip:** The recording will usually refer to all answer options. They may all be paraphrased but the details will not match. The wrong answers are known as distractors.

🎧 5

36
CD1

You are going to hear a reviewer talking about films. Listen and choose the correct answer a–c.

1 *What Happens in the Night* is based on
  a a story the director was told.
  b the director's childhood.
  c a comic book.

2 The reviewer thinks *What Happens in the Night* is
  a the best horror film this year.
  b visually stunning.
  c difficult to understand.

3 In real life, the stars of *Happy as Larry*
  a didn't get on.
  b fell in love.
  c are best friends.

4 The reviewer recommends you watch *Happy as Larry* if
  a you are a woman.
  b you like romantic films.
  c you liked Sonya's other films.

> ### *i* Exam information: Choosing answers from a list (2)
>
> As you saw in Unit 4, in the IELTS Listening exam, you may have to choose a number of correct answers from a list. You are likely to hear all the answer options, but only some of them will be correct; the other options will be incorrect in some way.

6 Read the question and the answer options a–e.

> How has fame changed?
> **a** More people are famous nowadays.
> **b** Talent is irrelevant in becoming famous.
> **c** The public now know almost everything about famous people.
> **d** Famous people have lost their mystery.
> **e** Fame is more short-lived.

The sentences i–v are examples of sentences you might hear on the recording. Read the sentences and decide which answer options a–e above are correct.

i Famous people have maintained their mystery.
ii People are now famous for only short periods.
iii It still takes immense talent to become famous.
iv Compared to the past, the number of celebrities has almost doubled.
v All aspects of a celebrity's life are made known to the public.

7 You are going to hear a writer talking about fame. Listen and answer the questions.

*37
CD1*

How has fame changed? List THREE ways from below.

a The public now know almost everything about famous people.
b Famous people have lost their mystery.
c More people are famous nowadays.
d Fame is more short-lived.
e Talent is irrelevant in becoming famous.

1 _____   2 _____   3 _____

Who are the 'losers' in fame? List THREE from below.

a Celebrities
b Photographers
c Executives
d The public
e Writers

4 _____   5 _____   6 _____

Part 3:   Exam practice

SECTION 2
QUESTIONS 1–3

38
CD1

Choose **THREE** letters **A–F**.

Give three reasons why the Yellow Plaque scheme was started.

  A   to boost tourism
  B   to raise awareness of local history
  C   to increase knowledge of famous people
  D   for publicity
  E   for architectural preservation
  F   to raise national awareness

1 _____   2 _____   3 _____

QUESTIONS 4–6

38
CD1

Choose the correct letter **A, B** or **C**.

4 The scheme has had the most success in
     A   increasing the amount of tourism in the area.
     B   raising the profiles of the famous people featured.
     C   raising historical awareness.

5 Successful Yellow Plaque nominees have to
     A   have a nomination and 50 signatures.
     B   be approved by a central panel.
     C   have done something remarkable.

6 The scheme is mainly funded by
     A   the community.
     B   local councils.
     C   the tourist board.

QUESTIONS 7–10

39
CD1

Match the plaques to the people they represent.

Write **ONE** letter **A–F** next to questions 7–10.

A	political figures
B	charitable figures
C	business people
D	sporting figures
E	artists
F	writers

7   Red Plaque _____

8   Grey Plaque _____

9   White Plaque _____

10 Green Plaque _____

7 Alternative energy

Aims: Reporting verbs | Identifying opinions and attitudes | Completing flow charts
Answering short questions | Completing sentences/summaries

Part 1: Vocabulary

1   The words below all relate to energy. Draw a table like the one below and put the words
     into the correct groups. Some words belong in more than one group.

boil	freeze	liquid	oil
burn	fuel	melt	oxygen
chemical	gas	metal	solar
cool	heat	nuclear	substance
electricity			

Noun	Verb	Adjective

2   Rewrite the sentences 1–8 by replacing the underlined phrases with words from Exercise 1.
     You can make other changes as well if necessary.

Example: In springtime the ice in the Arctic Circle <u>returns to a liquid state</u>.
In springtime the ice in the Arctic Circle melts.

   1   An effective way of producing power is to use energy <u>from the sun</u>.

   2   At the North and South Poles, water becomes so cold that it <u>changes from a liquid to a
       solid state</u>.

3   If you <u>raise the temperature of</u> water to 100 degrees Centigrade, it boils.

4   This power station uses energy <u>produced by atomic fission</u> to generate electricity.

5   Oil is <u>physical matter</u> found under the surface of the earth.

6   In order to make a fire, some kind of <u>combustible material</u> such as wood is needed.

7   If you <u>lubricate</u> an engine, it will function more effectively.

8   Refrigeration is the main method of <u>lowering the temperature</u> of food.

3   **Reported speech tells you what someone said, but does not use the person's actual words. These are modified and preceded by a reporting verb, which often also describes the function of their words.**

Example: 'I didn't copy my essay from another student.' → She <u>denied</u> copying her essay from another student.

Match the reporting verbs 1–10 with their meanings a–j.

1 warn ___	a to say that something is true or correct because you know about it
2 recommend ___	b to tell people about something publicly or officially
3 persuade ___	c to suggest that something should be done
4 announce ___	d to state that something is true and give the reasons why you think it is true
5 deny ___	e to tell someone about something such as a possible danger or problem so that they are aware of it
6 confirm ___	f to cause someone to do something by giving them good reasons for doing it
7 accuse ___	g to say something about someone or something, usually briefly
8 argue ___	h to say or tell someone that you believe they have done something wrong or dishonest
9 claim ___	i to state that something is not true
10 mention ___	j to say that someone else is saying something is true but you are not sure whether or not they are telling the truth

4   **The first sentence in each pair of sentences 1–5 is in direct speech, and the second is in reported speech. Complete the second sentence with the past simple tense of the correct reporting verb from Exercise 3.**

1   'We have found evidence that global warming is caused by human intervention in nature.'

Scientists _____ that they had found evidence that global warming was caused by human intervention in nature.

2   'The gas leak was not due to a broken pipe.'

The company representative _____ that the gas leak was due to a broken pipe.

3   'I think it would be a good idea to insulate your house to save energy.'

She _____ that they insulate their house to save energy.

4 'People have to change the way they think about using energy before it is too late for the planet.'

The environmentalist _____ that people had to change the way they thought about using energy before it was too late for the planet.

5 'Changing to green forms of energy will save you money in the future.' 'You are right. I will change.'

She _____ him to change to green forms of energy.

5 Complete the newspaper article with the words a–j.

a argued   d fossil   g recommended
b claim   e nuclear   h run out
c contamination   f radioactive waste   i solar power

> **The Future of Energy**
>
> The future of energy is changing. Scientists (1) _____ that (2) _____ fuels need to be replaced by alternative forms of energy. These older fuels, such as oil and gas, are in short supply and may (3) _____ in the near future. So what are the alternative forms of energy that could be used? (4) _____ is quite a popular choice for many. Harnessing the sun for its energy has been (5) _____ by the government's Department for Energy as a cost-effective and long-term solution for both businesses and individuals. However, although cost-effective in the long run, the setup costs can be high. Others have (6) _____ that (7) _____ energy would be a better solution. This, however, is very contentious. The issue of (8) _____ is always raised by its detractors because of the fear of (9) _____ if something goes wrong.

Part 2:   Practice exercises

> **Exam tip:** In the IELTS Listening exam, you need to be able to identify the opinions and attitudes of the speakers in conversations and understand if they agree or disagree with each other. Speakers can express their opinions and attitudes in various ways. For example, they may use an adjective that is positive or negative (e.g. *interesting, boring*), a verb (e.g. *agree, don't believe*) or a phrase (e.g. *That's what I think too, I'm not sure that's right*).

1 Read the phrases 1–10 and decide if the speaker is agreeing, disagreeing or expressing uncertainty. Write A (agreement), D (disagreement) or U (uncertainty).

1 I couldn't agree more. _____

2 Absolutely! _____

3 That's a difficult one. _____

4 I'm afraid I don't share your opinion. _____

5 This is where we differ. _____

6 There's no doubt about it. _____

7 I wouldn't like to say. _____

8 I'm not convinced … _____

9 I'm with you on that. _____

10 It's hard to say. _____

2 Read the dialogues and answer the questions 1–3. Then underline the words that helped you answer them.

Dialogue 1

A: I think we should visit the nuclear power station as part of our research for this module.

B: I couldn't agree more. And hopefully, we'll be able to interview some of the staff for a more in-depth view of how it works.

Dialogue 2

A: Geothermal energy is the best option for governments to invest in for the future.

B: Mm, I'm with you on that, but like all things it depends on the amount of investment.

Dialogue 3

A: What I particularly like about using hydrogen as energy is that it is environmentally friendly.

B: Well, I haven't seen any reports to support that so I wouldn't like to say.

1 Does the second speaker in dialogue 1 agree that they should visit the nuclear power station?

2 Do both speakers in dialogue 2 think that the government should invest in geothermal energy?

3 Do both speakers in dialogue 3 agree that hydrogen is environmentally friendly?

> **ⓘ** **Exam information: Flow chart completion (2)**
>
> A flow chart is designed to help people understand a process. It usually contains the key points or main ideas, rather than supporting points.

> **Exam tip:** When listening, it is important to identify which are the key points and which are the supporting points. Main points give general information, whereas supporting points give explanations and examples, or expand on something.

3 Read the list of safety instructions 1–6 for working in a laboratory and decide which are main ideas and which are supporting points. Write M (main idea) or S (supporting point).

1 Any food or drink containers found by staff should be disposed of. _____

2 Wear safety glasses and gloves at all times. _____

3 Do not eat or drink in the laboratory. _____

4 If you see an open door or window, please report it to security staff before working in the laboratory. _____

5 All doors and windows must be locked when leaving the laboratory. _____

6 If someone is not wearing safety glasses or gloves, ask them to put them on before continuing their work. _____

4 You are going to hear a tutor and a student discussing the process of doing a research project on alternative energy. Listen and complete the flow chart below. Write NO MORE THAN THREE WORDS AND/OR A NUMBER for each answer.

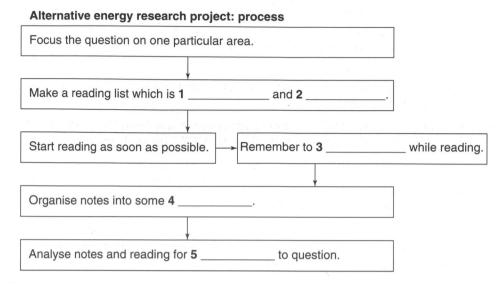

Alternative energy research project: process

Focus the question on one particular area.

↓

Make a reading list which is **1** _____ and **2** _____.

↓

Start reading as soon as possible. → Remember to **3** _____ while reading.

↓

Organise notes into some **4** _____.

↓

Analyse notes and reading for **5** _____ to question.

ℹ **Exam information: Short-answer questions (2)**

In some short-answer questions, you may have to identify two or three pieces of information. The question words include phrases such as 'List 2 reasons', 'Name 3 places ', 'Which 3 factors'. The answers are often close together in the recording and can be similar grammatically or thematically.

Exam tip: The question will help you focus on the type of answer you need to give in terms of grammar and topic so make sure you underline the key words in the question.

---

5 Read the questions 1–3 and underline the key words. Then decide what kind of answer is needed in terms of grammar and topic, and suggest possible answers. Write NO MORE THAN THREE WORDS AND/OR A NUMBER for each answer.

1 List 3 energy-saving methods.

_____ _____ _____

2 Name 2 substances which contribute to climate change?

_____ _____

Now listen and answer the question below.

3 List the 3 forms of energy Mary will write about in her essay. Write NO MORE THAN THREE WORDS AND/OR A NUMBER for each answer.

_____ _____ _____

Exam tip: In this type of short-answer question you will have to write one-, two- or three-word answers. If more than one word is required, think carefully about the grammar of your answer because it will need to be correct. You should think about the common grammatical combinations of words which will be tested, such as adjective + noun (e.g. *solar energy*), noun + noun (e.g. *power station*) verb + adverb (e.g. *decrease dramatically*) or verb + object (e.g. *improve the system*).

6 You are going to hear three students discussing their environmental science presentation. Listen and answer the question.

03
CD2

What 2 pieces of information do the students agree to remove from the presentation? Write NO MORE THAN THREE WORDS AND/OR A NUMBER for each answer.

1 _____   2 _____

i **Exam information: Summary completion (2)**

As you saw in Unit 4, in the IELTS Listening exam, you may have to complete a summary. Sometimes you have to choose the answers from a list of options in a box. There will be more options than you need.

Exam tip: In summary-completion tasks where you are given answer options, it is a good idea to identify which words are grammatically possible answers. That way, when you listen, you are choosing between a smaller number of options.

7 Which words a–l could complete the spaces 1–5 in the summary? There is more than one possible answer for each space.

a alternative	**d** dangers	**g** nuclear	**j** research
b benefits	**e** different	**h** price	**k** seminar
c cost effective	**f** evidence	**i** problems	**l** tutorial

The students are preparing for their (1) _____ discussion by discussing the various theories presented by academics in the field of (2) _____ energy. Overall, they agree with the academics that the most sustainable long term (3) _____ energy source is nuclear but they are concerned about the (4) _____ based on past disasters around the world. The students are unable to agree on the cost-to-benefit ratio of sources such as wind and solar because the academic (5) _____ appears to be inconclusive.

8 Now listen and complete the summary in Exercise 7 above with the correct words a–l. Write ONE option a–l next to 1–5 below.

04
CD2

a dangers	**d** cost effective	**g** different	**j** benefits
b price	**e** problems	**h** nuclear	**k** tutorial
c alternative	**f** evidence	**i** research	**l** seminar

1 _____   2 _____   3 _____   4 _____   5 _____

SECTION 3
QUESTIONS 1–4

05
CD2

Answer the questions below.

Write **NO MORE THAN THREE WORDS AND/OR A NUMBER** for each answer.

According to Phil, what are the 2 problems with some renewable energy sources?

1 _____

2 _____

List 2 things that Professor Jenkins wants to see in the students' report.

3 _____

4 _____

QUESTIONS 5–7

05
CD2

Complete the flow chart below.

Write **NO MORE THAN THREE WORDS AND/OR A NUMBER** for each answer.

Solar energy production costs forecast

Calculate the number of hours of **5** _____ in the UK.

↓

Estimate the number of hours of sunlight.

↓

Determine the cost of supplying homes in the entire **6** _____.

↓

Work out the power station construction costs.

↓

Research what customers would be **7** _____ pay.

QUESTIONS 8–10

Complete the summary below using words from the box.

Write **ONE** option **A–H** next to 8–10.

Project content summary

The alternative energy project will cover 3 main areas; a comparison, a price **8** _____ and an analysis. The students will use information given to them by their tutor and government **9** _____. Using a system of comparison between the data sets they will **10** _____ any discrepancies for further analysis.

A	data	**D**	demonstrate	**G**	reduction
B	highlight	**E**	prediction		
C	statistics	**F**	evaluate		

8 Migration

Part 1: Vocabulary

1 Match the words 1–12 with their definitions a–l.

1 census (*n*) ___	a all the qualities, traditions, or features of life of a country that have continued over many years and have been passed on from one generation to another
2 civilian (*n*) ___	b (of events) described or shown in the order in which they happened
3 demography (*n*) ___	c (of people or things) belonging to the country in which they are found, rather than coming there or being brought there from another country
4 indigenous (*adj*) ___	d a country which is controlled by a more powerful country
5 migration (*n*) ___	e the practice by which a powerful country directly controls less powerful countries and uses their resources to increase its own power and wealth
6 overpopulation (*n*) ___	f the study of the changes in numbers of births, deaths, marriages, and cases of disease in a community over a period of time
7 heritage (*n*) ___	g the problem that an area has when there are more people living there than can be supported properly
8 monarch (*n*) ___	h the movement (of people) from one place to another, especially in order to find work or to live somewhere for a short time

9 ancestors (n) ___	i an official survey of the population of a country that is carried out in order to find out how many people live there and to obtain details of such things as people's ages and jobs
10 chronologically (adv) ___	j anyone who is not a member of the armed forces
11 colony (n) ___	k the people from whom you are descended
12 colonialism (n) ___	l the king, queen, emperor, or empress of a country

2 Underline the correct word in italics in the sentences 1–6.

1 Human beings have been *migrating / migration* for many centuries for a variety of reasons.

2 The current *monarch / monarchy* of the UK is Queen Elizabeth II.

3 Mozambique is a former *colonialism / colony* of Portugal.

4 The traditions and culture of a country are part of its *inheritance / heritage*.

5 *Overpopulation / Overpopulated* is a major problem in many parts of the world.

6 *Demography / Demographic* information is useful when it comes to planning for the future.

3 Section 4 of the IELTS Listening exam is an academic-style lecture, in which the speaker often talks about how something has changed. This could be a change in appearance (making something look different), in quality (making something better or worse), or in quantity (making something more or less, bigger or smaller, etc.).

Read the sentences 1–10 and put the words in italics into the right groups, according to what kind of change they usually express. Some words fit in more than one group.

1 They were going to *restore* the building to its original state.

2 After recommendations from my boss, I *amended* the report.

3 The view of the government was *distorted* by the stories in the media.

4 The government *manipulated* the employment statistics.

5 The number of single parent families *boomed* in the 1990s.

6 The state of the economy *deteriorated* in the recession.

7 The number of healthcare professionals has *diminished* due to poor wages.

8 Poverty was almost *eradicated* with the introduction of welfare.

9 The number of immigrants *shrank* when the new act was introduced.

10 The value of the pound *tailed off* after the tax rise.

Change in appearance	Change in quality	Change in quantity

Part 2: Practice exercises

1 Knowing how words are pronounced in English is important in the IELTS Listening exam. One aspect of pronunciation is syllable stress. A word is made up of syllables (parts): for example, 'co-ffee' has two syllables, and 'im-por-tant' has three syllables. In English words, one syllable is stressed more than the others. For example, in '<u>co</u>-ffee' the first syllable is stressed, and in 'im-<u>por</u>-tant' the second syllable is stressed.

Underline the stressed syllable in the words 1–10. Then check in a good dictionary.

1	ci-vi-lian	**6**	he-ri-tage
2	de-mo-gra-phic	**7**	an-ces-tor
3	in-di-ge-nous	**8**	chro-no-lo-gi-cally
4	mi-gra-tion	**9**	co-lo-ny
5	po-pu-la-tion	**10**	co-lo-ni-al-is-m

> **Exam tip:** If there are some words on the answer paper that you do not know, practise saying the words in your head stressing different syllables before listening. This will help you to hear them on the recording.

2 As well as syllable stress on individual words, English also has sentence stress. Look at the following example:

<u>Listening</u> is an <u>important skill</u> for <u>studying</u> at <u>university</u> because you have to <u>listen</u> to <u>lectures</u> and <u>take</u> <u>notes</u>.

What types of words are stressed in the sentence above? For example, nouns, verbs, adjectives, articles, prepositions, connecting words.

Underline the stressed words in the sentences 1–5.

1 Due to the increasing number of people moving abroad for work purposes, home is something that is difficult to define.

2 One of the most important factors which causes people to move to a different city or country is employment.

3 Migration has been occurring since the beginning of humankind's habitation of the planet and is likely to continue for many generations to come.

4 The indigenous people of South America have not changed their way of life for centuries and continue to resist the effects of globalisation.

5 Our ancestors were nomadic people who moved from place to place in search of food and shelter.

> **ⓘ Exam information: Classification (2)**
>
> In a classification question, the options will be talked about in the order they appear in the question.

Exam tip: In classification questions, it is important to identify which set of options will be paraphrased: the A, B, C list, or the question list. You will hear the actual words of the list which is <u>not</u> paraphrased and this will help you match the lists. Lists containing names of people, places, countries, etc. are very likely to remain the same.

3 Look at the exam question below in which you are asked to match each family type 1–5 with the part of the city they live in a–c. Which list is more likely to be paraphrased, and why?

a	Eastgate
b	The Latin Quarter
c	Park Royal Gardens

1 Middle-class families _____
2 High-income couples with no children _____
3 Retired couples _____
4 Working-class families _____
5 Rich families _____

Now paraphrase each of the phrases 1–5.

1 _____   4 _____

2 _____   5 _____

3 _____

Exam tip: If the instructions are to write A, B, or C on the answer sheet, you must do just that. If you write the words, your answers will be marked incorrect.

4 Look at the exam question below and decide which information is likely to be paraphrased, a–c or 1–5. Think about ways to paraphrase the information before you listen.

07
CD2

You are going to hear a lecturer talking about resources for researching migration and family history. Listen and match the list of resources 1–5 with the types of access a–c in the box. Write a, b or c next to questions 1–5.

a	free to access
b	academic use only
c	requires payment

1 Family Records Centre and website _____
2 Genes Reunited _____
3 The National Census Association's statistical data _____
4 Journal of Historical Migration _____
5 Journal of Social Demography _____

ⓘ **Exam information: Labelling a diagram (2)**

Sometimes labelling a diagram will require you to relate information to a visual representation of the information you hear. The extent of the visual clues will vary.

Exam tip: When you are labelling a diagram, use the information given in order to prepare yourself for the recording. Firstly, notice how the numbers are arranged so you know in which order the information will be presented. Then look at the parts of the diagram that have already been labelled. You can use these as reference points while you are listening. Finally, try to understand the diagram by thinking about how the different parts relate to each other.

5 The diagram below illustrates the process of adapting to new cultures. Study the diagram and think about the order in which the information might be presented in a recording.

Put the list a–f in the order you think you would hear it on the recording. Use the information in the diagram to help you.

a External factors
b Negative internal factors
c Results

d Positive coping strategies
e Positive internal factors
f Negative coping strategies

___ ___ ___ ___ ___ ___

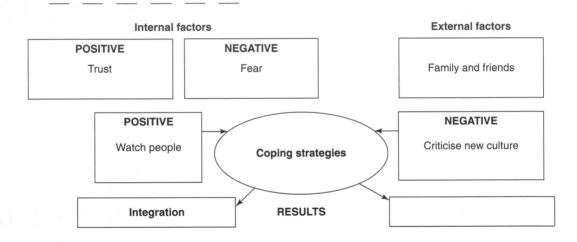

6 The diagram below illustrates the same process as the one in Exercise 5, but in a different way. Study the diagram and then listen and complete the spaces. Write NO MORE THAN THREE WORDS AND/OR A NUMBER for each answer.

08
CD2

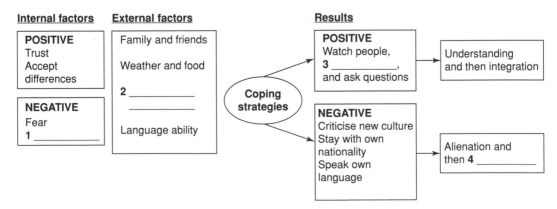

i **Exam information: Table completion (2)**

A table is a way of summarising information which can be categorised, e.g. date, price, time.

Exam tip: In table-completion questions, listening for the key words in the table will help you follow the recording. Remember that the answers will be in order on the recording but the information in the table may not. Having a good knowledge of English sentence structure will help you.

7 Look at the sentence below and underline the key words according to the table.

> The 1844 Naturalisation Act was designed to know more about immigrants as they had to give their personal information when they arrived in Britain.

Act and date	Reason for the act	Conditions to live in Britain
1844 Naturalisation Act	know more about immigrants	give personal information

Reorder the sentence fragments 1–3 below so that they form two new sentences that mean the same as the sentence above.

Fragment 1: they had to give their personal information under the 1844 Naturalisation Act
Fragment 2: so that the government could find out more about them
Fragment 3: when immigrants arrived in Britain

8 You are going to hear a lecturer talking about immigrants to Britain. Listen and complete the table. Write **NO MORE THAN THREE WORDS AND/OR A NUMBER** for each answer.

09
CD2

Act and date	Reason for the act	Conditions to live in Britain
1793 Aliens Act	control refugees from French Revolution	1 _____ on arrival
1844 Naturalisation Act 1870 Naturalisation Act	• know more about immigrants • regulate immigrants	• give personal information • resident for 2 _____
1914 Alien Registration Act	prevent 3 _____	register with police speak English
1948 4 _____ Act	encourage immigration for post war reconstruction	desire to work
1962 Commonwealth Immigration Act	restrict Commonwealth immigrants	obtain 5 _____

Part 3: Exam practice

SECTION 4
QUESTIONS 1–3

10
CD2

Label the diagram below.

Write **NO MORE THAN TWO WORDS AND/OR A NUMBER** for each answer.

Ellis Island immigration procedure

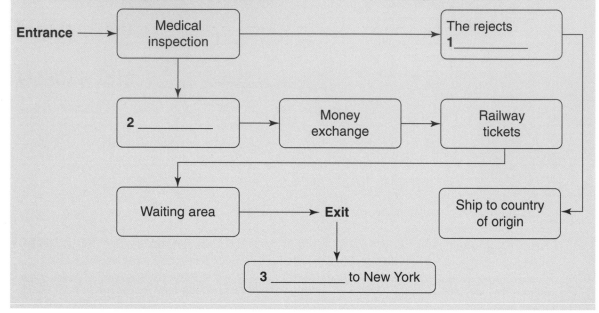

QUESTIONS 4–6

10
CD2

Match the areas of New York to the reasons affecting population change **A–D** in the box. Choose **ONE** option for each question 4–6.

A Political reasons	**4** Manhattan _____
B Economic reasons	**5** Brooklyn _____
C Employment reasons	**6** Queens _____
D Cultural reasons	

QUESTIONS 7–10

Complete the table below.

Write **NO MORE THAN TWO WORDS AND/OR A NUMBER** for each answer.

Brooklyn Case Study

	1900	1950	2000
Main economic activity	7 _____	Manufacturing	Financial services and construction
Population	1.5 million	2 million	8 _____
Transportation links	9 _____	Subway	Subway
Cultural Attractions	Coney Island amusement park	Development of the film industry	10 _____ of Prospect Park

9 At the gym

Aims: Using dependent prepositions | Moving on | Focusing on labels
Completing a form | Answering short questions | Labelling a diagram

Part 1: Vocabulary

1 Read about Steve's job in the gym and complete the spaces 1–5 with the correct form of the words a–f. Use each word only once.

a	recommend	**c**	health	**e**	instruct
b	fit	**d**	exercise	**f**	run

My name's Steve, and I'm the fitness
(1) _____ at the Aviary Place Gym. I love
my job as it's so diverse: one minute I'm making
(2) _____ to new members about which
classes to take, the next I'm (3) _____ one
of the many classes we have here. I mainly do
the boxing, spinning and aerobics classes. One
of the benefits is that it gives me a really
(4) _____ lifestyle. I'm constantly
(5) _____, which keeps me really
(6) _____. I wouldn't do any other job!

2 In Unit 4, we looked at verbs which are followed by prepositions (dependent prepositions). Some adjectives also have dependent prepositions.

Match the adjectives 1–8 with their definitions a–h. If the adjective has a dependent preposition, add it. Not all the adjectives have dependent prepositions.

1	predominant _____	a	unfriendly and aggressive, disagreeing with someone or disapproving of them, and often showing this in your behaviour
2	proportional _____	b	prevented from spreading beyond a particular place or group
3	confined _____	c	(of a state or level) the best that it could achieve
4	compatible _____	d	more important or noticeable than anything else in a set of people or things

5 optimum _____	e not affected by something
6 monotonous _____	f (of two amounts) increasing and decreasing at the same rate so there is always the same relationship between them
7 hostile _____	g very boring because it has a regular, repeated pattern which never changes
8 immune _____	h working well together or existing together successfully

3   Complete the text with adjectives from Exercise 2. The prepositions may help you.

Obesity occurs in many cultures, but it is (1) _____ in Western societies. However, the causes are probably lifestyle choices rather than genetic predisposition. Many westerners can control their weight and remain a manageable size; the amount of weight a person carries is usually (2) _____ to what foods they eat and how much exercise they do. People often find going to the gym a(n) (3) _____ task, involving hours at the treadmill or doing repetitive exercises, but there are other forms of exercise more (4) _____ with a person's disposition. Swimming, cycling and tennis are all good forms of exercise. Even if a person is slim, they should still do exercise. Being slim doesn't make a person (5) _____ to health problems which come from a lack of exercise. The (6) _____ amount of time to spend exercising per day is just one hour. Surely, that's manageable for everyone!

4   Here are three people talking about the gym. Complete the texts with the words a–e.

a coincided   **c** pinpoint   **e** stems
b incentive   **d** prompted

Jason: I saw myself in a photograph taken at a friend's wedding, and I almost didn't recognise myself. I had put on so much weight! That picture (1) _____ me to start coming to the gym more often. Now I go three times a week. I keep that picture by my front door as a(n) (2) _____ to keep exercising!

Andrew: My love of the gym (3) _____ from when I was eighteen and at university. I started going then, as I played in the university football team and wanted to stay fit. Well, I got bitten by the bug! That was ten years ago and since then I've been going to the gym every other day!

Eva: I can (4) _____ exactly when I started going to the gym. It (5) _____ with when I was recovering from a skiing accident. My legs often got stiff, and so I started going to the gym to try and ease this stiffness. It worked and now I love it!

Part 2:   Practice exercises

1   Underline the key words in the questions 1–5.

    1   Where was John born?
    2   Why does he love going to the gym?
    3   What time does he usually arrive at the gym?
    4   How often does he go to the gym?
    5   What unusual thing happened to him on his last visit?

2   Paraphrase the questions 1–5 in Exercise 1 above. Then put the topics a–e in the order in which you would probably hear them talked about according to the questions.

    a   Recent events
    b   Personal background
    c   Frequency of visits
    d   Motives for exercising
    e   Daily routine

    — —   — —   — —   — —   — —

> **Exam tip:** If you hear a speaker begin to talk about the next topic but you have not answered the question on the previous topic, do not waste time trying to answer that question. Instead, focus on the topic being talked about. The questions always follow the order of the information in the recording.

3   You are going to hear a conversation between two gym members. Listen and answer the
11   questions in Exercise 1. For this exercise only, there is no word limit. Two of the questions
CD2   will not be answered, so if you do not hear information about them, move on to the next questions when the topic of the conversation changes.

> ***i***   **Exam information: Labelling a diagram (3)**
>
> Diagrams show the relationships of parts, or how something works. Pictures or symbols may be used.

> **Exam tip:** In the IELTS Listening exam, you may be asked to label a picture. In such questions, it is important not to focus too much on the picture and how you yourself would describe it. Look carefully at those parts of the picture that *are* labelled to help you understand the *purpose* of the diagram, the *order of the information* and *how your answer will fit grammatically.*

4   Look at the picture of the gym equipment on page 75 and identify the purpose of the diagram, the order in which you will probably hear the information, and how your type of answer will fit in the labels grammatically. Then choose the correct option.

Purpose of the diagram:
    a   how to use a step machine
    b   the parts of a step machine

Flow (the order in which you will hear the points being talked about):

a   3 → wheel → 2 → spine → screen → 1 → grips
b   1 → spine → grips → 2 → wheel → 3
c   grips → 1 → spine → 2 → wheel → 3

Type of answer (you may choose more than one):

Question 1 will be: a noun / a verb / an adjective
Question 2 will be: a noun / a verb / an adjective
Question 3 will be: a noun / a verb / an adjective

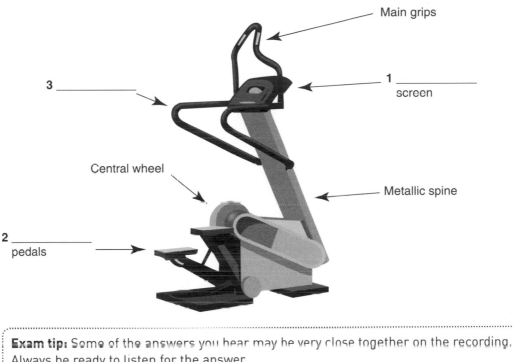

Main grips

3 _____

1 _____
screen

Central wheel

Metallic spine

2 _____
pedals

> **Exam tip:** Some of the answers you hear may be very close together on the recording. Always be ready to listen for the answer.

🎧 **5**   You are going to hear a conversation between a gym owner and an equipment salesman.
12   Listen and complete the diagram above. Write **NO MORE THAN TWO WORDS AND/OR A**
CD2   **NUMBER** for each answer.

> ℹ️ **Exam information: Form completion (3)**
>
> As you saw in Unit 1, in the IELTS Listening exam, you may have to complete a form. In Section 1, the information is factual, but sometimes form-completion exercises involve more complex information.

6 Look at the form below. Match the information required 1–8 with the type of answer you would have to listen for a–h.

JOINING THE GYM – FORM 3: FITNESS FORM

Name: Oliver Thompson

1 Contact number: _____

2 Age range: _____

3 Existing health conditions: _____

EXISTING EXERCISE REGIME

4 Frequency of exercise: _____

5 Types of exercise: _____

GYM EXERCISE ROUTINE

6 Reason for visits: _____

7 Frequency of visits: _____

8 Suggested workout: _____

a what kind(s) of exercise Oliver does now
b what kind(s) of exercise Oliver will do at the gym
c why Oliver wants to go to the gym
d what age group Oliver is in
e how often Oliver will exercise at the gym
f how often Oliver does exercise
g Oliver's telephone number
h what illnesses Oliver has now

7 You are going to hear a conversation between a receptionist at a gym and a client. Listen and complete the form. Write **NO MORE THAN TWO WORDS AND/OR A NUMBER** for each answer.

13
CD2

JOINING THE GYM – FORM 3: FITNESS FORM

Name:	Alice Watson
Age range:	16–25 (26–35) 36–49 50–59 60+
Existing health conditions:	1 _____
EXISTING EXERCISE REGIME	
Frequency of exercise:	twice a week
Types of exercise:	2 _____
GYM EXERCISE ROUTINE	
Reason for visits:	3 _____
Suggested workout:	Level 2 workout

> **ⓘ Exam information: Short-answer questions (3)**
>
> When answering a short question, you must always write the exact words you hear on the audio.

> **Exam tip:** In any question where you have to write the answer (for example, short-answer questions), it is essential to follow the instructions, be accurate in your written answer, and make sure the words you use are words from the recording. Details are important: you may lose marks if you do not read the instructions carefully or check your answers.

8 Read the questions 1–8 and a student's answers. Some answers are incorrect because the student did not follow the instructions or misunderstood the question. Match the incorrect answers given for questions 1, 3, 4, 5, 6 and 8 with the type of mistake a–f.

Questions	Answers
1 How often does the ladies' gym club meet?	*two times a week* (incorrect) _____
2 Where does the ladies' gym club meet?	*at reception*
3 What time does the aerobics class start?	*9.30 to 10.45* (incorrect) _____
4 Name three swimming instructors.	*Tom, Barbara* (incorrect) _____
5 Name two exercise classes running during the week.	*yoga, aerobics, circuits* (incorrect) _____
6 On what day is the next yoga class?	*Wednesday* (incorrect) _____
7 How long is the football training?	*three hours*
8 Why does the gym close early on Thursdays?	*7 p.m.* (incorrect) _____

a   incorrect spelling
b   too many words
c   too many answers

d   too few answers
e   misunderstood question
f   misunderstood question word

Now correct as many answers as you can.

🎧 **9**

14
CD2

You are going to hear two friends talking about the exercise classes they took in the last week. Listen and answer the questions 1–3. Write **NO MORE THAN THREE WORDS AND/OR A NUMBER** for each answer.

1 Which two classes did Debbie go to last week? _____

2 Why didn't Penny like yoga? _____

3 Where is Penny going next week? _____

Part 3:   Exam practice

SECTION 1
QUESTIONS 1–3

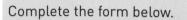

15
CD2

Complete the form below.

Write **NO MORE THAN THREE WORDS AND/OR A NUMBER** for each answer.

GYM MEMBERSHIP FORM

Name:	Brad Simmons
Telephone number:	**1** _____
Email address:	brad07@elemnet.com
Membership type:	**2** _____
Payment amount:	£36.50
INDUCTION DETAILS	
Date and time:	Saturday **3** _____ November at 2.30 p.m.
Trainer:	Rob Ellis

QUESTIONS 4–7

16
CD2

Complete the diagram below.

Write **NO MORE THAN THREE WORDS AND/OR A NUMBER** for each answer.

Diving board

7 _____

6 _____

Slow lane: Swim
anti-clockwise

4 _____:
Swim clockwise

Used by **5** _____ from
4 p.m. on weekdays

QUESTIONS 8–10

16
CD2

Complete the questions below.

Write **NO MORE THAN THREE WORDS AND/OR A NUMBER** for each answer.

8 Name two times that Brad will visit the gym: _____

9 What convinced Brad to choose Smith's gym? _____

10 What does Brad want to achieve at the gym? _____

10 At the office

Part 1: Vocabulary

🎧 **1**

17
CD2

In the IELTS Listening exam, it is important to know how to spell key words in the recordings. If you misspell a word in your answer, you will not get a mark.

Listen and underline the correct spelling of the words you hear (1–8).

1	reveniew	revenew	revenue
2	thrive	thraive	threive
3	comision	comission	commission
4	colaborate	collaborate	collaborrate
5	franchise	francise	franchaise
6	restructer	restructeur	restructure
7	ordit	awdit	audit
8	subsidury	subsidiary	subsidery

> **Exam tip:** When you record your answers, make sure your handwriting is clear. If it is not clear what word you have written, your answer will be marked incorrect.

2 Match the words in Exercise 1 with their definitions a–h below.

a to do well and be successful, healthy, or strong _____

b to change the way an organisation or system is organised, usually in order to make it work more effectively _____

c money that a company, organisation, or government receives from people _____

d to work together with a person or group, especially on a book or on some research _____

e a sum of money paid to a salesperson for every sale that he or she makes _____

f a company which is part of a larger and more important company _____

g an official examination of the accounts of a company by an accountant in order to make sure that they have been done correctly _____

h an authority that is given by an organisation to someone, allowing them to sell its goods or services or to take part in an activity which the organisation controls _____

3 Verbs which describe actions and processes are common in the IELTS Listening exam, and many of them have synonyms, which means they can be tested in many of the question types.

Match the verbs related to business 1–8 with their synonyms a–h.

1	optimise _____	a	continue
2	facilitate _____	b	choose
3	recruit _____	c	allow
4	proceed _____	d	settle
5	interact _____	e	maximise
6	opt _____	f	include
7	resolve _____	g	cooperate
8	incorporate _____	h	employ

4 Complete the text with words from Exercises 2 and 3, making sure the word form is grammatically correct. More than one answer may be possible.

So on today's programme, Business Matters, I'm talking about ways in which you can impress your boss and hopefully get that elusive promotion. Well, obvious as it may sound, demonstrating leadership skills and the ability to work in a team are two of the main ways to get yourself noticed. Your manager will be impressed if you can (1) _____ with others on projects, especially if this (2) _____ the company's profits or (3) _____. If you make sure your manager is aware of your strong points and the effort you have put into helping the company, you may be first in line for a promotion when your bosses decide to (4) _____ a department or the company. Another skill you should try to demonstrate to your boss is that of being able to (5) _____ problems or difficult situations. Many people naturally shy away from problems. If you can tackle them head-on, you make yourself valuable to your manager.

5 What is the difference between the pairs of words/phrases 1–6? Use a dictionary if necessary.

1 takeover, merger
2 turnover, profit
3 gross profit, net profit
4 copyright, trademark
5 marketing, advertising
6 go bankrupt, make someone redundant

6 The words 1–8 are all people who have some connection with business. Match the words with the definitions a–h.

1 stakeholder ____	a a person who is responsible for running part of or the whole of a business organisation
2 entrepreneur ____	b the person who got an institution, organisation, or building started or caused it to be built, often by providing the necessary money
3 founder ____	c a person who helps another person in their work
4 auditor ____	d the person or organisation that you work for
5 employer ____	e a person who has an interest in a company's or organisation's affairs
6 employee ____	f an accountant who officially examines the accounts of organisations
7 manager ____	g a person who sets up businesses and business deals
8 assistant ____	h a person who is paid to work for an organisation or for another person

7 Complete the sentences 1–6 with the correct form of the words 1–8 in Exercise 6.

1 Many _____ set up Internet businesses in the 1990s.

2 The _____ of Microsoft are Bill Gates and Paul Allen. They started the company in 1975.

3 The company has recently expanded and hired more _____.

4 Last week the _____ came to look at the financial records of the company.

5 In large organisations, people normally have their appraisal with their line _____ and a representative from Human Resources.

6 To set up a meeting with the director, please contact her _____ via email.

8 Match the verbs 1–8 with the nouns a–h to make common collocations to do with business.

1 restructure ____	a a contract
2 raise ____	b a team
3 file ____	c a department
4 minute ____	d a document
5 sign ____	e a meeting
6 send ____	f a point
7 close ____	g an email
8 lead ____	h a deal

9 Complete the conversation with the correct form of the collocations in Exercise 8.

Bob: Hi Sally, how are you?

Sally: Fine thanks, Bob. And you?

Bob: Fine. But I'm just a bit nervous today. I have to (1) _____ for an order worth hundreds of thousands. If I can get them to agree in general, all I'll have to do is work out a few details, and then we should be (2) _____ next week!

Sally: Oh, I'm sure you'll be fine. Just be your usual charming, persuasive self!

Bob: I'll try! As long as they don't (3) _____ which I haven't thought about.

Sally: I'm sure they won't. You should (4) _____ them _____ outlining all the points of the meeting before you arrive, just so there are no surprises. Oh, and make sure someone (5) _____ so that you have a clear record of everything that was discussed. And good luck!

Bob: Thanks!

Part 2: Practice exercises

1 In Unit 6 we looked at paraphrasing by substituting synonyms and changing word forms. In this unit we will look at paraphrasing positive and negative sentences:

Look at the following examples:

- Changing the verb from affirmative to negative or negative to affirmative:
  *The meeting **was difficult**.* → *The meeting **wasn't easy**.*

- *both ... and, neither ... nor*
  ***Both** Human Resources **and** the Finance Department **were unaffected** when the company was taken over.* → ***Neither** Human Resources **nor** the Finance Department **were affected** when the company was taken over.*

- *more than/less than*
  *Bob earns **more money than** Paul.* → *Paul earns **less money than** Bob.*

Paraphrase the sentences 1–5, but be careful not to change the meaning. Use the words in brackets to help you.

Example: The new software is more time-consuming than the old software. (time-efficient)
The new software is less time-efficient than the old software.

1 Working in a bank is less interesting than working in a hotel. (more interesting)

_____

2 Neither managers nor staff in the catering industry earn high salaries. (both / low)

_____

3 Most of the company's employees have little experience in IT. (only a few)

_____

4 The staff kitchen is usually dirty. (often / clean)

_____

5 The meeting was managed badly. (wasn't / well)

_____

2   Another way to paraphrase information is to change the order of the words in a sentence. This can be done in various ways. Look at the following examples:

The company pays commission to its sales staff. → *The sales staff are paid commission by the company.*

Most people want to gain promotion at work so they can progress in their careers. → *In order to progress in their careers, most people want to gain promotion.*

Managing a team can be a rewarding experience. → *Managing a team can be an experience which is rewarding.*

Paraphrase the sentences 1–4.

1   An outside accounting company audits their finances.

_____ are audited _____.

2   Although the travel industry sounds glamorous, it involves working long hours.

_____ although it _____.

3   Designing modern office buildings is a challenging task.

Designing _____ which is _____.

4   The managers warned their employees about impending job losses.

Employees _____ by their managers.

ⓘ   **Exam information: Table completion (3)**

Tables often have headings which identify the information categories needed in the answers.

---

3   In table-completion questions, accuracy is very important; your answers are likely to be marked incorrect if you write a singular noun instead of a plural noun, or an adverb instead of an adjective.

Look at the tables and decide which of the options, a or b, are more likely to complete 1–6 correctly.

1 Company name	2 Product	3 Suitable for
a The Youthful Travel Company	a an adventure holiday	a young people
b The Youthfully Travel Company	b adventure holidays	b young person

4 Department name	5 Main work	6 Location
a Finance	a responsible for company accounts	a in a city centre
b Financial	b responsibly for company accounts	b in the city centre

🎧 **4** You are going to hear someone talking about a department restructure and the other
18
CD2 changes in the company. Listen and complete the questions 1–3 in the table. Write NO
MORE THAN THREE WORDS AND/OR A NUMBER for each answer.

Sales Team	Human Resources Team	Product Development Team	IT Support Team
Gary Wilson	Linda French	Zoe Green	Ian Smith
• Increase business with existing clients • Find new clients	• Recruit 20 new sales staff • Appoint an internal **1** _____ to the manager of each team	• Research competitor products • Create 2 new product **2** _____ this year	• Ensure all clients receive follow up calls • Improve package for **3** _____

ⓘ **Exam information: Summary completion (3)**

Summaries are shortened versions of information. They usually focus on key points
and less on details.

Exam tip: In summary-completion questions, it can be difficult to listen and read the
text at the same time. Remember that the summary will contain key points or main
ideas rather than details, and that synonyms will often be used. This means that words
and phrases in the summary text *and* on the recording are likely to be synonyms.
Before you listen, it is a good idea to underline the words you think may be replaced by
synonyms to prepare for the recording. As you listen, focus on the synonyms and the
words between them which are likely to be the answers.

5 Look at the words and phrases a–g in italics in the summary below and think of as many
synonyms for them, words and/or phrases, as you can.

> ### Fire evacuation summary
>
> If the fire alarm (a) *is activated*, all staff should (b) *make their way to* the main stairs
> unless it sounds at 11.00 a.m. on a Tuesday, in which case it is (1) _____. Do not
> waste time by picking up any bags or (2) _____. (c) *Once outside* the building,
> staff should follow the (3) _____, who will (d) *direct them to* the waiting area at
> the back of the building. Each department has an appointed fire safety officer (e) *who
> is responsible for* checking all their staff have (f) *left* the office. This person must then
> report any (4) _____ to the fire safety manager. The fire safety manager will
> notify people when it is (g) *safe to return.*

Exam tip: You need to listen and read the text at the same time in the IELTS Listening
exam. Before you listen, it is a good idea to underline the words you think may be
paraphrased. This will help prepare you to listen more efficiently.

🎧 **6** Listen and complete the summary.

19
CD2

> **Fire evacuation summary**
>
> If the fire alarm is activated, all staff should exit the building using the main stairs unless it sounds at 11.00 a.m. on a Tuesday, in which case it is (1) _____. Do not waste time by picking up any bags or (2) _____. Once outside the building, staff should follow the (3) _____, who will direct them to the waiting area at the back of the building. Each department has an appointed fire safety officer who is responsible for checking all their staff have left the office. This person must then report any (4) _____ to the fire safety manager. The fire safety manager will notify people when it is safe to return.

ⓘ **Exam information: Classification (3)**

Classification questions always have two sets of information: the classification groups, and the items to be classified.

Exam tip: Rephrasing the categories in the classification box and the numbered list to make a question can be useful. When you turn classification information into a direct question, it can help you focus on the key points in the recording.

---

7 Look at the question below.

Who in the office is responsible for the tasks in 1–4?

a	Sarah
b	Brian
c	Helen

1 Orders all stationery   _____

2 Makes reservations for meeting rooms   _____

3 Sends weekly email updates to all staff   _____

4 Liaises with the cleaning staff   _____

Now look at the question based on the information in a, b and c, and number 1.

Example: Which person, Sarah, Brian or Helen, orders all the stationery in the office?

Make similar questions for 2–4.

🎧 **8** You are going to hear a marketing manager talking to his staff. Use the question-making technique you learned in Exercise 7 and prepare to listen to the recording.

20
CD2

Now listen and answer questions 1–4.

Which advertising methods will the company be using for its different products?

a	Newspapers
b	Television
c	Internet

1 Children's toys   _____

2 Baby clothes   _____

3 Maternity clothes   _____

4 Baby food   _____

Part 3:   Exam practice

SECTION 2
QUESTIONS 1–3

🎧 21 CD2

Complete the table below. **WRITE NO MORE THAN THREE WORDS AND/OR A NUMBER** for each answer.

Overview of Benchmark Consulting

2000	Founded by James Cox	First office in Melbourne	Established new 1 _____
2006	Fred Montgomery	Opened the Perth office	Increased revenue to 2 _____
2008	Sold to TFB Group Ltd for $10 million	Created new 3 _____ in Sydney	Contract with Australian government

QUESTIONS 4–6

🎧 22 CD2

In which city **A–C** are the company's functions in 4–6 located?

A Sydney
B Perth
C Melbourne

4   Marketing _____

5   Staff training _____

6   Administration _____

QUESTIONS 7–10

🎧 22 CD2

Complete the summary below. **WRITE NO MORE THAN THREE WORDS AND/OR A NUMBER** for each answer.

Benchmark Consulting – company vision for the future

Over the next five years, Benchmark Consulting will create two **7** _____ companies in order to increase business with European and Asian organisations. In all departments, more **8** _____ will be recruited over the next year, and to ensure Benchmark Consulting is a good choice for potential employees, salaries for staff will be raised by **9** _____. Staff who will have to move to a different city following the restructure will receive a **10** _____ to assist with expenses.

11 Local languages

Part 1: Vocabulary

1 Match the words 1–10 with their definitions a–j.

1	eloquent _____	a	an imaginative way of describing something by referring to something else which is the same in a particular way. For example, if you want to say that someone is very shy and frightened of things, you might say that they are a mouse.
2	epigram _____	b	good at speaking and able to persuade people
3	idiom _____	c	words, expressions, and meanings that are informal and are used by people who know each other very well or who have the same interests
4	illiterate _____	d	a long speech which is spoken by one person as an entertainment, or as part of an entertainment such as a play
5	jargon _____	e	a group of words which have a different meaning when used together from the one they would have if you took the meaning of each word separately
6	metaphor _____	f	unable to express yourself easily or well in speech
7	monologue _____	g	short saying or poem which expresses an idea in a very clever and amusing way.
8	nuance _____	h	words and expressions that are used in special or technical ways by particular groups of people, often making the language difficult to understand
9	slang _____	i	not knowing how to read or write
10	inarticulate _____	j	a small difference in sound, feeling, appearance, or meaning

2 Match the words connected to language 1–6 to the examples a–f.

1 language _____	a It's raining cats and dogs.
2 dialect _____	b Cockney
3 slang _____	c German
4 idiom _____	d America is a melting pot.
5 metaphor _____	e Happy birthday
6 collocation _____	f Our holiday was <u>dead good</u>.

3 Underline the correct word in the sentences 1–6.

1 A(n) *dialect / accent* is a form of a language that is spoken in a particular area.
2 People who cannot hear use *sign language / semaphore* to communicate.
3 *Rhetoric / Metaphor* is the skill or art of using language effectively.
4 The *nuances / connotations* of a word are the ideas or qualities which it makes you think of.
5 A *transcription / tracing* of a conversation or speech is a written text of it, based on a recording or notes.
6 A person who is *bilingual / illiterate* can speak two languages equally well, usually because they learned both languages as a child.

4 In Unit 7 we looked at phrases for agreeing and disagreeing. However, sometimes people use certain adjectives or adverbs to express their opinion, and this is another way of understanding if speakers agree or disagree.

Read the dialogue and underline the adjectives or adverbs that express opinion.

Angela: I thought the lecture on UK regional accents had some credible points about the ways in which English is changing.

Kevin: To be honest, I'm a little sceptical of some of the evidence. It seemed to me that their predictions were insufficiently detailed.

Angela: Really? I thought the research methodology appeared to be logical. Maybe the researchers were just cautious with their predictions for the future of English.

Now answer the questions 1–3.

1 Do Kevin and Angela agree?
2 Who had a positive reaction to the lecture and who was more negative?
3 Which adjectives and adverbs helped you answer questions 1 and 2?

5 Are the adjectives and adverbs of opinion 1–10 positive or negative? Write P (positive) or N (negative) next to each one.

1 viable _____	5 erroneous _____	9 deceptive _____
2 flawed _____	6 compelling _____	10 reliable _____
3 rigorously _____	7 needlessly _____	
4 authentic _____	8 succinctly _____	

> **Exam tip:** When you learn new adjectives and adverbs, make sure you know they are used positively or negatively.

Part 2: Practice exercises

1 *(CD2 23)* In Unit 8 we saw how content words such as nouns, verbs, adjectives and adverbs are usually stressed in English. English also has weak forms – words that are not stressed in speech. These words include auxiliary verbs (e.g. *be, have, do*), prepositions (e.g. *in, at, of*), pronouns (e.g. *my, us, your*), articles (*a, an, the*) and conjunctions (e.g. *and, but, so*).

Read the examples below and then listen. Notice how the underlined words in each sentence are more difficult to hear than the words in italics.

- When I <u>was</u> *living* <u>in</u> *Ireland,* <u>it was</u> *quite difficult* <u>to</u> *understand* <u>the</u> *local accent.*
- <u>Do you</u> *think* <u>it's</u> *important* <u>to</u> *sound* <u>like a</u> *native speaker?*
- I <u>would have</u> *learnt Latin* <u>but it wasn't an</u> *option* <u>when I was at</u> *school.*

(CD2 24) Listen and complete the sentences 1–3 with words from the recording. They are all weak forms.

1 Many _____ dialects _____ world _____ gradually dying out.

2 _____ recommend ways _____ which I _____ improve _____ listening skills?

3 _____ researching minority languages _____ essay _____ I went _____ British library _____ find out more information.

2 *(CD2 25)* In English it can be difficult to understand natural speech because the words sound as if they are connected.

Listen to the sentence below. Does it sound more natural the first time you hear it or the second time?

Learning a language isn't easy.

When a word ends in a consonant sound (e.g. *d, k, t, z*) and the next begins with a vowel sound (*a, e, i, o, u*), English speakers usually connect the words.

There‿are lots‿of‿uncommon languages‿in‿Europe.

(CD2 26) Now listen to the sentences 1–2 and mark (‿) where the words are connected.

1 There are many South American Indian languages, none of which are related to Spanish.
2 Studying accents is a good way to understand if a language is changing or not.

3 Another feature of connected speech in English is when one word ends in the same consonant that the next word begins with. The first consonant disappears.

Catalan i$ spoke// nowadays by many of the youn// generation.

(CD2 27) Now listen to the sentences 1–2 and mark where the sounds disappear.

1 I stopped taking Greek lessons soon after I left school.
2 How will local languages stay in use if fewer people learn them?

> ℹ **Exam information: Multiple choice (3)**
>
> In the IELTS Listening exam, some of the multiple-choice questions require you to choose the correct answer from a set of diagrams or pictures. For this type of multiple-choice question, it is important that you understand what the diagrams or pictures show and try to predict how they will be described before you listen.

4 Look at the pie chart concerning minority languages in the UK and answer the questions 1–4.

Number of UK speakers in % in 2010

🔲 Welsh
▨ Gaelic
⬜ Cornish
⬛ Irish

1 Does the pie chart show the number of speakers or the percentage of speakers?

2 Which countries are shown in the pie chart?

3 Does the pie chart refer to the recent past, the distant past, or both?

4 Match the languages a–d to the proportions i–iv.

a Welsh _____
b Gaelic _____
c Cornish _____
d Irish _____

i the smallest percentage
ii around ten per cent
iii about a quarter
iv over half

5 You are going to hear a group of students discussing minority languages in the UK. Listen and answer the question below.

🎧 28 CD2

Which pie chart, a, b, or c shows the correct percentage of speakers of UK minority languages?

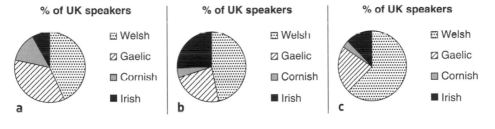

% of UK speakers

🔲 Welsh
▨ Gaelic
⬜ Cornish
⬛ Irish

a

% of UK speakers

🔲 Welsh
▨ Gaelic
⬜ Cornish
⬛ Irish

b

% of UK speakers

🔲 Welsh
▨ Gaelic
⬜ Cornish
⬛ Irish

c

i **Exam information: Labelling a map or plan (3)**

Maps or plans include plans of buildings, maps of countries or cities, roadmaps, and area plans amongst others.

6 In Units 2 and 5, we looked at locations and directions for labelling a map or plan. This unit focuses on geographical positions.

Match the positions on the map 1–6 with the descriptions of geographical position a–f.

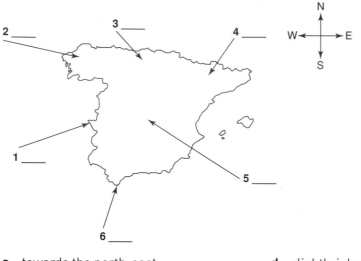

a towards the north-east	**d** slightly inland from the north coast
b at the southernmost point	**e** in the far north-west corner
c along the west coast	**f** in the interior

7 You are going to hear a group of students discussing their presentation on the languages of the different regions of Spain. Listen and label the map.

29
CD2

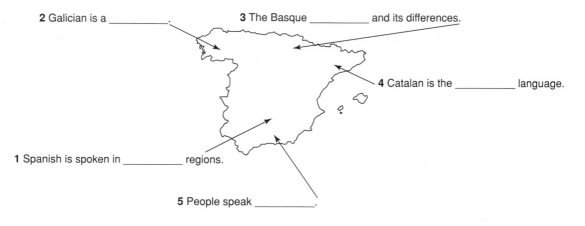

2 Galician is a _____.

3 The Basque _____ and its differences.

4 Catalan is the _____ language.

1 Spanish is spoken in _____ regions.

5 People speak _____.

> **ⓘ** **Exam information: Selecting from a list**
>
> In the IELTS Listening exam, this type of question is sometimes simple. For example: 'Name 3 reasons ...' or 'Choose 2 factors ...'. In these questions there is more detailed information in the list of options. However, this can be reversed so that the question contains more detail and the options are simple.

8 Look at the question below and notice how most of the detail is in the question. It is likely that the answers will be referred to in words that are different from those in the list.

> Which of the following ways of encouraging people to speak local languages does the tutor recommend that the students should include in their report?
>
> **1** Education   **3** Clubs   **5** Music
> **2** Business   **4** Social networking

Match the words 1–5 with a–e.

1 Education ____	a songs which are popular with young people
2 Business ____	b places where people who share the same hobbies can meet
3 Clubs ____	c courses offered at primary and secondary schools
4 Social networking ____	d work done by companies for commercial profit
5 Music ____	e discussion groups which take place in an online setting

> **Exam tip:** Remember to check how many marks are awarded in this question type: there may be one mark for each correct answer or one mark if all the answers are correct.

30
CD2

9 You are going to hear a discussion between a tutor and two students about an assignment. Listen to and answer the question.

Which TWO of the following ways of encouraging people to speak local languages does the tutor recommend that the students should include in their report? Write a–e.

> **a** Education   _____
> **b** Business   _____
> **c** Clubs
> **d** Social networking
> **e** Music

Exam tip: At the end of the IELTS Listening exam, you have ten minutes to transfer your answers from the exam booklet to the answer sheet. Make sure you do this carefully: do not write the answers in the wrong spaces or you will lose marks. Only the answers on the answer sheet are marked.

SECTION 3
QUESTIONS 1–2

31
CD2

Answer the questions 1–2.

1   Which countries are the students going to visit for the field trip? Choose **A**, **B** or **C**.

   A the United States of America and Canada

   B Mexico and the United States of America

   C Canada and Mexico

2   Which of the graphs below correctly shows the numbers of people under 25 years of age who speak three languages? Choose **A**, **B** or **C**.

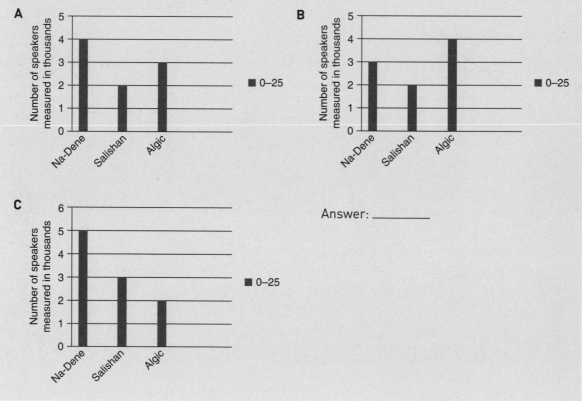

Answer: _____

QUESTIONS 3–6

Which four social factors affecting native-language usage do the students want to research during their field trip?

Choose FOUR letters from **A–F** below.

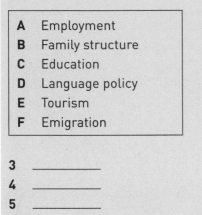

A	Employment
B	Family structure
C	Education
D	Language policy
E	Tourism
F	Emigration

3 _____

4 _____

5 _____

6 _____

QUESTIONS 7–10

Label the map below.

Write **NO MORE THAN THREE WORDS AND/OR A NUMBER** for each answer.

Proposed field trip itinerary

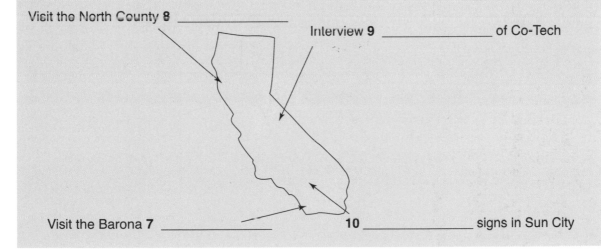

Visit the North County **8** _____

Interview **9** _____ of Co-Tech

Visit the Barona **7** _____

10 _____ signs in Sun City

12 Practice test

33
CD2

*Answer the questions below. Choose the correct letter, **A, B** or **C**.*

1 Why does Ellen want some new clothes?

   A for her holiday

   B for her new job

   C for her brother's wedding

2 Which dress does Ellen want to buy?

   A   **B**   **C**

3 Which hat does Ellen decide to buy?

   A   **B**   **C**

 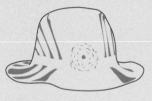

QUESTIONS 4–7

33
CD2

Complete the form below. Write **NO MORE THAN THREE WORDS AND/OR A NUMBER** *for each answer.*

	Delivery Form
Name:	Ellen Barker
Delivery address:	**4** _____
	Staybridge
	Kent
	DA4 7DF
Telephone Number:	**5** _____
Delivery date:	12th May
Delivery time:	**6** _____
Payment type:	Visa
Amount:	**7** £_____

QUESTIONS 8–10

34
CD2

Complete the plan below. Write **NO MORE THAN THREE WORDS AND/OR A NUMBER** *for each answer.*

Department store layout:

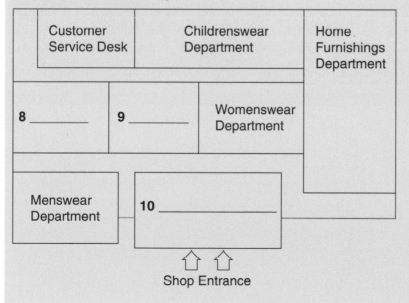

SECTION 2
QUESTIONS 11–13

Answer the questions below. Write **NO MORE THAN THREE WORDS AND/OR A NUMBER** *for each answer.*

11   When does the tour finish? _____

12   Which area is not shown on the tour? _____

13   Which landmark does the tour guide recommend the tourists should visit?
_____

QUESTIONS 14–17

Match the activities with the group they are recommended for. Write **A–C** *next to* **14–17**.

A	Families
B	Elderly couples
C	Young people

14   Dinner cruise   _____

15   Climbing wall   _____

16   Coastal walking tour   _____

17   Wine tour   _____

QUESTIONS 18–20

36
CD2

Complete the flow chart below. Write **NO MORE THAN TWO WORDS AND/OR A NUMBER** *for each answer.*

Getting an Explorer Pass:

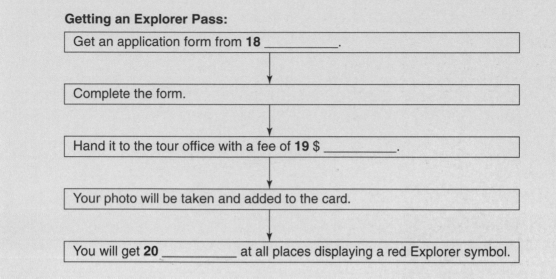

Get an application form from **18** _____.

↓

Complete the form.

↓

Hand it to the tour office with a fee of **19** $ _____.

↓

Your photo will be taken and added to the card.

↓

You will get **20** _____ at all places displaying a red Explorer symbol.

SECTION 3
QUESTIONS 21–23

37
CD2

Complete the notes below. Write **NO MORE THAN TWO WORDS AND/OR A NUMBER** *for each answer.*

Presentation focus: **21** _____ animals

Presentation time: 20 minutes

Pros: Plenty of **22** _____ for the presentation; interesting subject

Cons: Difficult to **23** _____

QUESTIONS 24–26

🎧 37 CD2

Choose **THREE** *letters A–G.*

Which **THREE** *ways does the tutor suggest Katie and Ian can improve their presentation?*

A   Do their research on the Internet

B   Limit the amount of detail within the presentation

C   Separate the presentation into clearer sections

D   Use some video clips

E   Focus on only a selection of animals

F   Make sure they practise the presentation

G   Think of some discussion questions for the audience

24   _____

25   _____

26   _____ G _____

QUESTIONS 27–30

🎧 38 CD2

Complete the diagram below. Write **NO MORE THAN TWO WORDS AND/OR A NUMBER** *for each answer.*

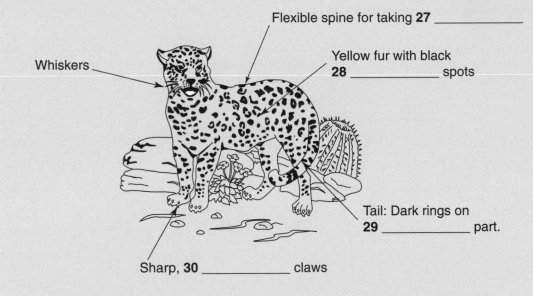

Flexible spine for taking 27 _____

Yellow fur with black 28 _____ spots

Whiskers

Tail: Dark rings on 29 _____ part.

Sharp, 30 _____ claws

SECTION 4
QUESTIONS 31–34

39
CD2

*Complete the summary below. Write **NO MORE THAN THREE WORDS AND/OR A NUMBER** for each answer.*

> **SUNDIALS**
>
> With the sundial, daylight was measured in twelve **31** _____ which were longer and shorter depending on the seasons. The first known sundial is a **32** _____ sundial from Egypt. After some development, sundials could measure time accurately despite seasonal changes and **33** _____. People have sundials today as **34** _____ items in their gardens.

QUESTIONS 35–37

39
CD2

*Answer the questions below. Write **NO MORE THAN THREE WORDS AND/OR A NUMBER** for each answer.*

35 For whom were mechanical clocks <u>not</u> originally built? _____

36 What reason is given for having a standardised time? _____

37 Where are the atomic clocks kept? _____

QUESTIONS 38–40

39
CD2

*Choose **THREE** letters A–F.*

*Match the following book titles with the recommendations in **A–F**.*

A	Gives a good general overview
B	Covers concepts of time in different cultures
C	Is the most essential text
D	Looks at more philosophical aspects
E	Provides more in-depth analysis
F	Covers modern time technology

38 Understanding Time _____

39 Time: Concepts and Conventions _____

40 The Story of Time _____

Audio scripts

The underlined sections of the audio scripts indicate where the answers to questions can be found.

CD 1

Track 01

Steve:	Hey, Jenny!
Jenny:	Oh, hi, Steve. Nice to see you.
Steve:	Good to see you, too. How's it going?
Jenny:	Fine, thanks. I'm so glad the exams have finished.
Steve:	Me too. So, are you going on holiday this summer?
Jenny:	Yes, I've decided to go to Mexico for the whole summer vacation, six weeks in total.
Steve:	That sounds great! What are you going to do there?
Jenny:	Well, actually, it's a working holiday. I'm going to work at a school teaching English to children. What about you?
Steve:	I'm going to Paris for two weeks.
Jenny:	Are you going with your family?
Steve:	No, I'm going with my best friend. We've enrolled in a language school to study French.
Jenny:	That sounds like fun. Have a good trip.
Steve:	You too.

Track 02

Reception:	Good afternoon. Royal Mount Hotel. How may I help you?
Customer:	Hello ... Er, I'd like to book a twin room, please, for next week.
Reception:	One minute, please ... I'll just check if we have one available. ... Yes, we do, sir. Now, I just need to take down a few details, if I may.
Customer:	Yes, of course.
Reception:	What name is the booking under?
Customer:	My name ... Duncan Geoffrey. That's G–E–O–double F–R–E–Y.
Reception:	G–E–O–double F–R–E–Y. Aha. And could I have a contact telephone number, please?
Customer:	Yes, 5762 23821.
Reception:	When will you be arriving, sir?
Customer:	Some time on the evening of the nineteenth.
Reception:	Of September?
Customer:	Yes, and we'll be leaving on the twenty-third. How much will that be in total?
Reception:	So ... That's a twin room ... For a twin, it would normally be £235, but I can give you a special rate as it's low season: £210 for the four nights.
Customer:	Great. Thank you.
Reception:	And how would you like to pay, sir? We accept cash, cheque or credit card.
Customer:	I'll pay cash on arrival, if that's OK.
Reception:	Of course, sir. We look forward to seeing you.

Track 03

Customer:	So, what are the differences between these four hotels?
Travel agent:	Well the main difference is in the facilities they offer. The Hotel Sunshine is the only one which has a gym and it's also got one of the top health spas in the area. It's next to a lake so you can do water sports there. But if you *really* like sailing or waterskiing, then the Highland Hotel would probably be the best place because it offers great instruction programmes in these sports.
Customer:	Actually, I'm not a sporty person.
Travel agent:	OK. Well, what about the Hotel Carminia? It's a brand new hotel, and it prides itself on its cinema and multimedia centre. And then there's The Royal. This one has a conference room, a meeting room, and free computer access, but it's not really appropriate for children; there's not much in the way of entertainment.

Customer:	Well, I'm going on holiday, not to work, and it's just my wife and me so I think we'll book with the Hotel Carminia, please.

Track 04

Sam:	So, there's a great walking tour tomorrow morning. Or tomorrow night we could go on the cruise round the harbour. What do you think, John?
John:	Well, we've got theatre tickets for tonight, so we'll be too tired for the walking tour in the morning. But I don't fancy the cruise, either.
Sam:	Why not? It'll be fun! Look, it's a dinner cruise, and it's only $12 each.
John:	I hate the sea, and I'll be sick with fear if the waves are big! And dinner ... on a boat ... I just couldn't.
Sam:	But we'll be in the harbour!
John:	Still ... Ah, but what about this? There's a bus tour tomorrow evening. It's only $5.50 and it goes all around the main tourist sites!
Sam:	Yeah, that sounds OK ... [fade]

Track 05

John:	Where shall we eat tonight?
Sam:	Well, there are plenty of options. The guide says this city has hundreds of restaurants. What kind of food would you like to have, John?
John:	Well, I quite like seafood. There's The Captain's Table on Firth Street. The guide gives it four stars.
Sam:	I don't know ... The hotel receptionist told me the service is slow. But if you like seafood, there are a couple more places in the guide.
John:	Ah, yes ... Mangan's or Joe's Café. What about those, Sam?
Sam:	Mangan's could be a good option. It's nicer than Joe's Café, and there are fantastic views as well. We'd probably pay a bit extra ... Joe's Café is much cheaper. But we're on holiday; I think we should splash out!
John:	That sounds great! Oh, no. Hold on. It's closed tonight. What a shame! Shall we go to Joe's Café, then?
Sam:	Yes, I suppose we'll have to. I'll give them a call and book a table. Can I use your phone?
John:	Ah, er ... no. Sorry. I've left my phone in the hotel. We can ask the receptionist to do it. Let's go back now and sort it out. We can get changed and have a drink before dinner if you like.
Sam:	OK, good idea

Track 06

Tourist office assistant:	Hello, how can I help you?
Tourist:	Um, hello. Is it possible to book a bus tour of the city here?
TOA:	Of course, sir. When would you like to take the tour? There are tours in the morning, afternoon, and evening ... sometimes it's nice to see the city at night with the buildings lit up.
Tourist:	We'll be going out for dinner tonight, so we'd prefer to go this afternoon. Oh, and it's for two people.
TOA:	Right. Now I just need some details. Can you give me the names of the two people, please?
Tourist:	Yes. Susan Field and James Carter.
TOA:	Susan Field and James – sorry, can you spell your surname for me, please?
Tourist:	It's Carter. C–A–R–T–E–R.
TOA:	Thank you. And can I have a contact telephone number?
Tourist:	Why do you need one?
TOA:	Just in case we have to cancel the tour and need to contact you.
Tourist:	I see. Well, my mobile number is 07988 636197 (0–7–9–double 8–6–3–6–1–9–7).
TOA:	That's 07988 636197. Now, can you also tell me which hotel you're staying at?
Tourist:	The Crest Hotel. Oh no, sorry. That's the hotel we're staying in next week. It's the Riverside Hotel.
TOA:	Oh! The Riverside is a lovely hotel. Are you enjoying your stay?
Tourist:	Yes, we are, very much. We'd definitely recommend it to others.
TOA:	Oh I am glad. Now, I can book you on the tour at 4 p.m. Would that suit you? Alternatively, there is one at two.
Tourist:	Two would be better for us, please.

TOA:	Right, that's booked for you, sir. <u>Two people at 2 p.m. today, August 14th</u>. You pay the bus driver when you get on, and it's £4 per person.
Tourist:	Thank you very much.

Track 07

Tourist:	Can I also ask you about the museum in the main square? I was reading about it in my guide book and was shocked to see that the entrance price is £10. Why does it cost so much?
Tourist office assistant:	Well, the museum has the largest collection of Latin American art in Europe. People come from all over the world to see it. But that's not the reason why it's so expensive to get in. You see, the building is very old and it needs repairs. <u>The £10 ticket cost will go towards repairing the roof and the walls.</u>
Tourist:	I see. Well, I suppose it's worth paying £10 to see the collection.
TOA:	Yes, I think so too. Is there anything else I can help you with?
Tourist:	Actually, there is. I was wondering if you knew of any good restaurants in the area.
TOA:	Well, there are a few restaurants near the harbour, and a couple on the beach which are nice. The problem is that the smell of the fish market is quite strong down there.
Tourist:	Mm, I don't think my girlfriend would be very pleased.
TOA:	I know what you mean – it's not very romantic, is it? My advice would be to go to the next town. <u>It's bigger, and the restaurant selection is wider.</u> You can get there by taxi and it only takes about ten minutes. The town is quite picturesque ... Is it for a special occasion?
Tourist:	Yes, it's my girlfriend's birthday so I'd like to go somewhere special. Um, do you know any of these restaurants well enough to tell me about them?
TOA:	Well, I know about a few of them, and there are pictures in this leaflet here. <u>This one here is lovely – the Belleview – and it's extremely popular. It has a famous chef, so it's not cheap, but the standard of the food is very high.</u> It's right by the sea and there are wonderful views if you get a good table. Then there's The Lighthouse Café – you can see the picture here – which isn't really a café at all. <u>In fact, it's a great restaurant and a lot of TV celebrities and actors eat there.</u> The place has been going for over a hundred years! It's quite an institution around here.
Tourist:	Mm. I'm not sure about those two – they sound too expensive to me. I was thinking of somewhere small, not too up-market, but with good food.
TOA:	In that case what about Harvey's? <u>The same family has run this restaurant for over a century,</u> and it's reasonably priced and really popular with local people. <u>And there's another family-run restaurant, Stonecroft House. New owners took over a month ago and they're getting good reviews.</u> There's a new chef there and the food is meant to be very good. This leaflet has the contact details for all the restaurants so you can just call them if you'd like to book a table.
Tourist:	Great, thanks. You've been very helpful.

Track 08

Dance school manager:	Hello, everyone. Sorry to interrupt your class. I just want to make a quick announcement about our summer timetable. Shimmers Dance School will be offering new classes this spring due to strong demand. <u>Angela Stevenson will be back this term, running the ballet class.</u> This class will be on Tuesdays, and instead of the normal hour from 6.30 to 7.30, we'll be running the class for an hour and a half, so it will continue until 8 o'clock. <u>This means we have to charge higher fees, but only slightly higher: from £8.50 (eight pounds fifty) to £10.50.</u> That's only £2.00 for the extra half hour! Next, <u>Janine Davis will still be teaching the tango classes. Instead of being on Mondays these classes will be on Wednesday nights from 7 o'clock to 8 o'clock.</u> The fee will still be £7.50 for the hour. Last but not least, <u>Andrew is taking over the tap class. This class is for early risers as it starts at 8.30 on Saturday morning and finishes at 10.</u> We expect this class to be very popular as tap is a great way to get fit while learning new dancing skills. This will cost £11.00. All the other classes remain the same as the winter timetable. We hope there's something for all of you at Shimmers!

Track 09

Man:　Internet safety is a big concern nowadays and to protect your children and teenagers online, it's a good idea to monitor the sites they visit. Don't be put off from letting your kids use the Internet; it's essential for their education and can help them make friends too!

Now, let me tell you a bit about some sites we've found for children. Of course, there's a limited number of sites for the very young, but we would suggest one called Playtime Online. It's designed for children from four to six years old. It's really colourful and helps children learn skills for games. Children love it and it helps them when they begin school. Then, from say five until about ten years of age, there's a really useful website called Moving Up. This takes Playtime Online a step further and enhances the maths and language skills of the child. Teachers speak highly of this site for child development.

When children get into their teens, the Internet can be a more dangerous place. Net Aware, for the twelve to sixteen year age group, makes young people more aware of online dangers. It's a good site for your child to look at before they start surfing on their own.

Now, all teenagers love chatting, and Chat Electric is a site designed specifically for teens from thirteen to sixteen to make friends online with people their own age.

The last site is invaluable for teens studying for exams. Sixteen- to eighteen-year-olds love Test Doctors, which is a site designed to help students revise for their exams and is full of handy hints and tips. The site is run by subject specialists so it's packed full of information.

Track 10

Camp manager:　The Health and Action Summer Camp in the county of Cork in southern Ireland is ideal for young people who would like to learn new sports and activities. It has a beautiful location near a river and occupies five acres.

The camp has two types of accommodation; tents and cabins, both of which are modern and comfortable. The cabins are by the river and the tents are on higher ground, away from the river and next to the wash rooms. There are two washroom blocks, fully equipped with showers as well as toilets.

We also have facilities for cooking here. We provide all the pots, pans and utensils. All cooking is done in the cooking area, which is situated in the centre of the camp. This gives the camp a real social focal point.

Track 11

Woman:　The Duke of Edinburgh's Award is a programme of activities designed to help young people from all backgrounds develop personally. There are three levels: Bronze, Silver and Gold, and for each level participants have to complete a series of activities in four categories: volunteering, physical, skills, and expedition.

This talk will explain what you have to do in order to get a Bronze award. The first thing you need to do is find a Duke of Edinburgh centre near you. This could be your school, college, or youth club. Then you'll need to pay a small fee to enrol in the programme. Once you've enrolled, you'll get a welcome pack which explains the four categories in more detail. Then you can start planning what to do. You can do many different types of activity for each category, but you must get them approved by your Duke of Edinburgh Coordinator before you start so you don't waste time doing something which is not approved. The other important person is your assessor. This is the person who will certify that you've completed each activity by signing your record book. After you've completed all the activities in the time given, your assessor will send your record book results to the operating authority, who will check it. If everything is satisfactory, you'll get your certificate and badge to confirm you've completed the award. And after that, you can start working on the Silver award!

Track 12

Leisure centre manager:　Good morning, everyone, and thank you for coming to find out more about the new Teen Programme here at the Park Hill Leisure Centre. I'd like to take you through the programme, the classes available, describe the building itself, and then give you some information about how to register and sign up for the sports and activities we offer. Afterwards, you'll have an opportunity to take a tour of the centre. We also have some taster sessions with our instructors, which we hope you'll enjoy, and which will motivate you to sign up!

Let's go through the classes first. As you can see from the Teen Programme handout in your pack, we have lots of classes on offer. Our instructors are highly qualified and have lots of experience training young people. Diana is our dance instructor, and she gives classes in jazz and salsa on Wednesday and Thursday evenings respectively. Jim usually takes the football practice sessions, but this year he is branching out into American sports and will be running the baseball club on Saturday afternoons. We think this will be very popular. So Steve will now run the football practice. This class has been changed from Saturday to Sunday afternoons. Steve will also take the skateboarding class on Monday evening. The roller-skating course is for beginners, and this will be taken by Stella, who was last year's under-21 London roller-skating champion, so you'll be in good hands with her expert advice. The day of this course is still to be arranged but it's likely to be Tuesday. We'll confirm the day by the end of this week.

Track 13

Leisure centre manager: Now some of you won't have been to Park Hill Leisure Centre before, so let me just tell you a little about the layout. As you can see, the reception area here is very spacious, and there is plenty of room to meet your friends and have a drink. We also have brand-new dance studios with floor-to-ceiling mirrors and the latest audio equipment. The dance studios are to the left of the reception area, behind the swimming pool. No ... sorry ... I meant opposite the swimming pool. Both the roller skating and skateboarding classes will be held in the Skate Arena. This has also been refurbished and we have a new five-metre ramp in there which is proving to be popular. The arena is behind the changing rooms, which you can see behind us, between the gym and tennis courts. The tennis courts are on the right of the arena. You'll see both of these new spaces on the tour later.

Now, the final thing I want to talk about is how to join the Park Hill Leisure Centre and enrol for the classes. First you need to complete an enrolment form with some of your personal details, including your address and telephone number and the name of your school. If you're under sixteen years old, then you'll also be required to get your parents' permission to take part in the classes. Please ask one of your parents to sign the authorisation form attached to the enrolment form. You'll find the form in your information pack. When you've done this, you just hand the forms to reception. You can pay an annual subscription of twenty pounds, or alternatively, you can pay each time you use the facilities. There is a one pound sixty admission fee in this case. Whether you decide to pay in one go or with each visit, you still need to complete the forms in your pack and become a member. Once we have the forms, we'll send your membership card to your home address. All you need to do is show this card every time you come to the centre, and if you want to book a class, you just need your membership number on your card.

Track 14

1 glaciers
It is assumed that glaciers move slowly, but occasionally they have surges and move up to fifty times faster than normal.

2 salinity
The Dead Sea is famous for the salinity of its water.

3 humidity
The humidity in tropical areas can make you very tired.

4 kilometres
The oceans can reach depths of eleven kilometres in places.

5 pressure
Altitude sickness is due to a reduction in air pressure.

6 evaporation
Rain is mainly caused by evaporation from the oceans.

7 environment
We need to look after the environment around us.

8 biology
Biology is a branch of the natural sciences.

9 brightness
Our perception of the brightness of the sun changes with the seasons.

Track 15

Linda:	Hi, everyone. How are you all?
John:	I'm fine thanks, Linda.
Steven:	Actually, I'm not feeling so well – I think I've got a cold.
Linda:	Oh no, Steven. I'm sorry to hear that. What about you, Joanne?
Joanne:	I'm fine, but I'm very busy with my biology course.
John:	Oh, me, too – there's so much work to do.
Joanne:	In that case, we should get started on our essay. John, do you want to start?
John:	OK ... Let me start by telling you my ideas for the essay.

Track 16

Alice:	We've really got to decide who does what for our Natural Earth project.
Karl:	OK, Alice. Well, we've got all our cloud research so let's decide how to break it down.
Alice:	Well, we should probably start by saying how clouds are formed.
Karl:	Good idea, and then maybe move on to the different types of clouds. We can separate it into low-lying, medium-level and high clouds. What do you think, Jenny?
Jenny:	Yes, I think that's a good idea, and we should also make a PowerPoint to make it a bit more interesting, and put in pictures of the different clouds.
Alice:	Good idea, Jenny! We should probably have cue cards, too. I'm useless at remembering what to say without them!
Karl:	Yes, me too! Well, I'm quite happy to organise everything we've found out about clouds and make sure it fits into our presentation times.
Alice:	Actually, I'd better do that. I've got all the research on my computer so it makes sense. How about if you make the presentation slides, Karl?
Karl:	OK, Alice. That's fine by me.
Jenny:	Well, if you guys are going to do that, then I'll look on the Internet for pictures of the different types of clouds.
Alice:	That'll be great, Jenny. I'll also make the prompt cards so we don't forget what we're saying during the presentation.
Karl:	Sounds great. Let's have a run through on Tuesday. What sections does everyone want to talk about? I don't really mind.
Alice:	I hate speaking in front of people so I'd prefer not to do the introduction.
Jenny:	I don't mind, I'll do that. If you don't want to talk much, then why don't you just do the middle bit about the medium-level clouds?
Karl:	Yes, I can do the low-level and high-level clouds part. I'm sure Jenny can handle the summarising, too.
Alice:	Thanks, guys. We can all take questions together.

Track 17

Debbie:	Hi, Roger.
Roger:	Debbie! Hi. How are you?
Debbie:	Oh ... I've been struggling with my Natural Earth assignment. It's proving to be really difficult.
Roger:	The one for Professor Black? Me too. I'm writing about volcanic activity. What are you doing yours on?
Debbie:	Acid rain. I thought that would be OK, but the process is really complicated.
Roger:	Well, I can help you with it! I know a lot about acid rain. I studied the causes and effects last year.

Debbie: Really? That's great ... I've done some work on the causes. I'm going to write that acid rain is caused by sulphur dioxide from power plants and smelters. Basically, this reacts in the atmosphere to form acid rain.

Roger: Ah, but it's not just sulphur dioxide, it's also nitrogen oxides.

Debbie: Really?

Roger: Yes, from things like car exhausts.

Debbie: But aren't nitrogen oxides also caused by natural events, too?

Roger: Yes. They're a minor factor, but I think they're worth mentioning. But, sorry, carry on ...

Debbie: Thanks. I might add that. So anyway, these emissions react in the atmosphere with water, oxygen and oxidants to form acidic compounds like sulphuric acid. These compounds then fall to earth.

Roger: Are you going to mention the different ways they return to the ground?

Debbie: Do you mean wet and dry deposition?

Roger: Yes! So you've done a bit of background reading, then?

Debbie: Yes ... so if I've got it right, acid rain often comes down as rain, but also as snow or fog. This is wet deposition. I'm also going to define it as any form of precipitation that removes acids from the atmosphere.

Roger: Yes, I think that's a good term to define it.

Debbie: Dry deposition, ... Well, I think that's when the pollutants stick to the ground through dust. I'm not really sure how to define it, though, compared to wet deposition.

Roger: Just think of it as any pollutants that are not caused through precipitation. That's probably the best way. Did you know that sunlight can enhance the effects of acid rain as well?

Debbie: No, I didn't. There's so much to think about. I'm sure I'll go over my word limit.

Roger: Well, you sound like you know a lot about the subject. Just try and keep your focus. I've had the same problem writing about volcanoes! There's just so much!

Track 18

Charlotte: Do you want to make a start on our Natural Earth project? I think our idea of a lightning safety presentation is great, don't you, Rachel?

Rachel: Yes, I think it'll be really good ... I have a few ideas already.

Charlotte: Great! Me too. I think we should divide it into two parts: what to do if you're inside when lightning strikes, and what to do if you're outside. What do you think?

Rachel: That's good, but we need more. Something about planning for this kind of event. And also, what to do if someone gets hit by lightning.

Charlotte: I can't believe I forgot that! Of course! Well, what should we talk about in the first part?

Rachel: I think we should say it's important to be aware. Lightning is always before rain, so don't wait until it rains. As soon as you hear thunder or lightning you should get inside.

Charlotte: OK, yes. And then if you're indoors, you should avoid water. Stay away from doors and windows, and don't use the telephone.

Rachel: Or any electrical equipment. In fact, if you can, switch it off first. And you should wait half an hour after the last clap of thunder before going back outside.

Charlotte: And if you're outside when it storms, you also need to avoid water. Try and get inside as soon as possible. There are certain things you should avoid ... open spaces ... anything large and made of metal. And of course the obvious one: trees.

Rachel: But we should mention that if lightning strikes very near you, you need to crouch down.

Charlotte: Oh! Is that right? I thought you had to stand still.

Rachel: No, that's actually wrong – you're supposed to crouch down ...

Charlotte: ... and put your hands over your ears. The noise can damage your hearing if you don't. OK ... I think we've got quite a lot here. Only the last part to go. Now: what to do if someone gets hit.

Rachel: I think we should say that it's very rare for someone to get hit by lightning. Our talk sounds as if there's danger all around! We should try and make it sound a bit more reassuring!

Charlotte: Yes, you're right – we'll say it doesn't happen often. It's just better to be safe than sorry. But what should we say about getting hit by lightning?

Rachel: Well, I think we should say it's safe to touch people who've been hit by lightning ... they don't have any electrical charge! If there's a first aider around, then they should help them. Otherwise it's just best to call for an ambulance. <u>And we should remind our audience that eighty per cent of lightning victims don't get fatally injured!</u> That should calm everyone's nerves!

Track 19

Emma: So, I think we'd better start planning what we're going to do for our group project. Have you guys had any ideas?

Tom: I was thinking we should do something on extreme weather events, but I think Alex had some different ideas.

Alex: <u>Yes, maybe we should look into more localised weather conditions and the effects on the immediate environment.</u>

Emma: <u>That's a good idea, Alex, but I don't think we'd be able to get much data on that, and we don't really have time to do our own research.</u> What about doing something about the seasons?

Tom: <u>I think the seasons might be a bit too wide-reaching,</u> you know, when we take into account the wind patterns and pressure systems.

Emma: Maybe you're right.

Alex: <u>Well, how about Tom's idea of extreme weather conditions?</u>

Emma: <u>Yes, that sounds like a good idea. It's easy to break down into separate parts and it certainly sounds more interesting!</u>

Tom: I'd quite like to cover monsoons. I've been doing some reading on them and they're quite interesting.

Emma: Well, that sounds good. We should maybe take two areas each – that would make it easier for us to focus.

Alex: Well, we've got lots to choose from: we could do blizzards, heat waves, droughts, cyclones. There are loads! Why don't you do blizzards too, Tom?

Tom: <u>I don't fancy doing them, but I wouldn't mind doing something on floods.</u> They're linked to monsoons, I think, so it will be an easy transition. What do you fancy doing, Alex?

Alex: Well, I could always cover winds.

Emma: But that isn't really extreme enough.

Alex: <u>Hmm ... I could do hurricanes, they're pretty exciting.</u> How about doing cyclones, Emma?

Emma: <u>I'd rather do heat waves and droughts, I think.</u> I know a bit about them. I don't know anything about cyclones.

Alex: <u>Cyclones are really interesting. I can cover them.</u>

Tom: That sounds great. I was thinking about doing cyclones, but I'm happy for you to do them.

Track 20

Emma: Right, shall we get started on some of the content?

Tom: Yes, we haven't got that much time. Does anyone know anything about their topics?

Alex: I know quite a lot about cyclones.

Tom: Do you?

Alex: Well, I studied them at high school. You know, cyclones usually start near the equator. They need quite warm water to form. <u>Above the warm water, the vapour in the air forms clouds, and if there is low pressure, then these clouds will start to rotate.</u>

Tom: Isn't it also the fact that the earth rotates too which makes the clouds spin more?

Alex: Yes, that too. <u>Once they begin rotating, they can either lose momentum or keep gathering momentum until they hit land</u> – these ones are called mature cyclones. Luckily, as soon as they hit land, they start to lose momentum and fade away. Just because they don't have the warmth of the ocean underneath.

Emma: Well, that's a relief!

Alex: They can still be really destructive. They're like a big circle of wind. They blow strongly until the eye of the storm passes – you know, the centre, where everything is really quiet, no wind or anything. <u>But then the other side hits and the winds blow just as strongly but in the other direction!</u> It's just amazing! Yes, I would really like to cover that.

Emma: Well, it looks like we've got it all arranged, then!

Track 21

Jenny: My family isn't very big. There's just my son and me. I'm a single parent. For the last ten years I've been concentrating on looking after my son James, who is now fourteen. But now I've met someone special and we've just got engaged! My fiancé has four kids of his own and we're going to get married in July. James is really excited about it; he's looking forward to having brothers and sisters in his new step-family!

Sheila: We live as one big extended family. There are seven of us in our household. Besides my husband and me and our children, there's my aunt and two of my cousins. I stay at home and care for my mother because she's quite old and can't look after herself. Obviously, we suffer from a lack of space in the house, but we all get on well.

Track 22

1 Firstly, I am going to talk about the role of the parent. Secondly, I'll discuss the role of the child, and lastly, we'll look at the family unit as a whole.
2 Parenting is a difficult job because no two children are ever the same.
3 Families are important because they form the basis for socialisation. Additionally, they educate and protect the next generation.
4 The family structure has varied greatly over time. That is, different times have had different views of what a traditional family structure is.
5 Many argue that less traditional structures are not as effective. However, there is little evidence to support this.
6 Many people are having families later in life. Consequently, the rise in the number of single people may only be temporary.
7 Families in other parts of the world differ from the western norm. For instance, in some cultures having multiple husbands or wives is the norm.
8 Although there are many arguments for trying to keep the traditional family structure strong, I feel the key issue is the economic necessity of having a 'normal' family structure.

Track 23

Lecturer: As we have seen, changes in the structure of the family are constantly occurring: extended to nuclear, patrifocal to a more equal footing between the sexes, and dual parenting to single parenting. However, a recent phenomenon in the UK which is changing the traditional family is the increasing number of adults who continue to live with their parents until their thirties or sometimes even their forties. The UK has traditionally been a society where offspring leave the family home in their late teens or early twenties to set up their own home and families. But in the last twenty-five years this has decreased. Official statistics released by the Office of National Statistics show that today ten per cent of men in their early thirties still live with their parents; this compares with five per cent of women in this age range.

The reasons for this are complex and varied. It cannot be denied that some people are choosing to stay at home. Living with parents can be an easy option; food is provided, heating and electricity are paid for, and rent, if any, is minimal. However, a third of those surveyed claimed they are living with their parents because it is too difficult to get on the property ladder. House prices in the last few decades have risen dramatically; property is now five times the average annual salary, whereas it was only three times the average annual wage in the 1980s. This fact, coupled with high unemployment amongst young people, makes it virtually impossible for a single person to buy a home or even rent.

The number of students going on to higher education has also been steadily increasing. Many of these students return home after finishing their studies as a result of the student debt they have accumulated. It can take many years to pay this off, and if the burden of rent or a mortgage is added to that, it can be just too much for a young adult's pocket.

However, help is now at hand. The government is tackling some of the problems that cause people to remain with their parents with a new scheme: the Affordable Housing Scheme. This aims to help people part buy a house or flat by making housing more affordable for first-time buyers, and possibly taking the strain away from elderly parents!

Track 24

Lecturer: The family is a topic which we will look at in great detail this term. For sociologists, the family is often seen as the beginning of socialisation. Indeed, it is the seed of society itself. In recent decades, many old people have no longer been able to rely on their offspring for support, which was common fifty years ago. Many children are brought up by only one parent, something virtually unheard of before the 1960s. <u>We can certainly say that during the last half century we have seen an enormous change in traditional family structures</u>.

The extended family lasted well into the early 1900s, and <u>this kind of strong family unit was essential due to property ownership</u>. Housing often was scarce and it was necessary for people to live with parents and take over the property when their parents died. Of course, people still benefit from their family line. <u>Still today, people generally inherit any money that their mother or father might have</u>.

In the UK, the last fifty years has also seen a decrease in the number of offspring parents have. Whereas in the 1950s only ten per cent of offspring were only children, this number has risen. <u>Nowadays, this is the case for just over a third of children</u>.

Track 25

Lecturer: In Victorian times, the upper classes made up less than three per cent of the entire population of Britain, yet this class held more than ninety per cent of the country's wealth. This shows the massive gap there was between rich and poor, a gap which has shrunk considerably in the last century. Today we're going to look at the wide differences in family life between rich and poor in Victorian times. Let's begin with the upper classes.

The upper classes of the Victorian period were generally the nobility or the clergy. <u>Most of their servants were very poorly paid, but were always accommodated within the homes of upper-class Victorian families, so they didn't have to pay for accommodation, food and often clothing</u>. The money which they did earn, they normally sent home to their families.

Many Victorian servants came from the countryside, where the effects of the industrial revolution had resulted in job losses. Amongst these servants were cooks, housemaids, stable hands, and butlers. The family would also employ a nanny, who although employed by the family, was not traditionally seen as a servant. A nanny's primary role was to care for the children. She was responsible for teaching the children how to behave, looking after them when they were ill, and instilling discipline into them. Nannies did not, however, educate the children. <u>Generally, children from wealthy families did not attend school outside the family home. Tutors would come to the house to do this</u>, and although <u>on occasion mothers taught their children to read and fathers gave their children some instruction in Latin</u>, this was not a common occurrence.

Now, the Victorian upper classes have the reputation of being quite cruel; but this wasn't always the case. <u>They were also quite charitable. Ragged schools were set up with funding from the upper classes so that poor children could have some form of education</u>. Additionally, most Victorian parents were very proud of their children, who were often seen as 'prized possessions'. <u>This goes against the common idea that parents were very hard on their children. In fact, the opposite was generally the rule</u>. However, the situation for lower class families was very different. In the lower classes child labour was rife. Children as young as eight earned a living as chimney sweeps for wealthy houses.

Now, let's move on to looking at the lower class families in more detail. You'll find that ...

Track 26

Lecturer: We are all familiar with the nuclear family, which has been the dominant family structure in the UK for the last sixty years at least. <u>However, recent changes show that our idea of the traditional nuclear family as the cornerstone of British family life is changing</u>. There have been emerging patterns which are eroding this structure; namely, the rise of step-families, cohabitation, lone-parenting, and the rapid increase in those living alone. We are going to explore these areas in turn, and look at their effect in terms of the family.

Firstly, step-families are becoming more and more common. Step-families are created when one or both partners have a child or children from a previous relationship. In 1980 the percentage of children under thirteen who were living with one parent and their new partner was just four per cent. In 2008, this figure had increased to twenty per cent. <u>The USA has seen an even greater rise; new statistics show that almost half of under thirteens are living in a step-family</u>. Now, we can still call the step-family structure a 'nuclear' family, as it does follow the structure of two parents, and dependent children. However, it also creates somewhat of a nuclear 'blur'. Step-brothers and sisters may belong to two family units, so where do we draw the line at which family they belong to?

Co-habitation, when partners do not marry yet live together as a family, has also increased. In 2006, of the 17.5 million families in Britain, nearly three million of these comprised unmarried couples. What does this mean to the nuclear family? Firstly, the traditional view of a nuclear family requires married parents, so we can't put these types of family under this umbrella. Statistics show that even if cohabiting couples have children, they are more likely to separate than their married equivalents. Lastly, we need to look at the rise of the DINKS, which stands for Dual Income No Kids. As Clarke and Henwood outline, many cohabiting couples are choosing a life without children, putting consumer spending first.

Lone-parenting is a relatively recent family structure which has rapidly grown in the last half century. In 1972 only one in fourteen children lived in a lone-parent family. When we compare this with today's figure of one in four, we can see that this is a rapid increase. In the past, lone-parenthood was overwhelmingly the result of a death of a parent. Nowadays however, it is increasingly a choice. Some sociologists argue that this increase is due to the outlook of women. Where women once were willing to accept an unhappy or abusive marriage, now many will choose lone-parenthood. Often this can be just a transitory phase before they find a new partner. This view of women's attitudes and lone parenting is highly debated, because some figures show that the largest group of lone parents are mothers who have never married. You can find counter arguments for these ideas in Butler and Jones.

One difficulty for single parents is that they are a social group who are much more likely to suffer from poverty and hardship. They are more likely to live in rented accommodation and have childcare issues.

Lastly, an increasing number of people are choosing to live alone. The number of people living alone in Britain has more than doubled in the last twenty years. In 1990 just over four million people lived alone. Now this figure has reached 8.5 million, an incredibly rapid growth which has had enormous effects on the traditional nuclear family. This number represents a great chunk of the population who either by choice or necessity, are outside the traditional family unit. Some think that these changes may not help the community. In fact, there are many arguments that this rise in alternative household structures will create a more isolationist and less community-based society, where close bonds which are usually formed within the family have no place. Leaving aside whether or not the housing even exists for this boom, an important factor which must be looked at is the disproportionate expense for those living on their own. By this I mean, the burden of all costs is shouldered by one wage instead of two, and of course one person is using the energy which could be shared between a group, having a greater impact on the environment too.

However, on a more positive note, people, especially women, are proving . . .

Track 27

Sally:	Hi, Dad. How are you?
Father:	I'm fine, Sally. How's the course going?
Sally:	It's going well, actually. I'm really enjoying my math course at the moment, mainly because it's not that difficult compared to the other modules.
Father:	Good. And what about the tutors – what are they like?
Sally:	Well, I've got four, and they're all highly knowledgeable, but Professor Jones is my favourite – I really respond well to the way he teaches.
Father:	And are your fellow students nice, too?
Sally:	Yes, I've made lots of new friends and everyone seems to be very hard-working. The course has lots of group work, but to be honest, this isn't really the way I like to study – I prefer to study alone.
Father:	Oh, well, I suppose not everything can be perfect.
Sally:	I know, Dad, you're right. In fact, there is one thing I'm a bit concerned about. My statistics module. I think I might not pass it.
Father:	Well, let's wait and see, shall we – there's plenty of time to improve. Don't worry about it yet, OK?
Sally:	Thanks, Dad, I'll try not to.

Track 28

a

A:	Excuse me, can you tell me where the bank is, please?
B:	It's opposite the cinema, next to the supermarket.

b
A: Excuse me, can you tell me where the bank is, please?
B: It's round the corner from the supermarket.

c
A: Excuse me, can you tell me where the bank is, please?
B: It's up the road from the supermarket beside the cinema.

d
A: Excuse me, can you tell me where the bank is, please?
B: It's at the opposite end of the street from the cinema.

e
A: Excuse me, can you tell me where the bank is, please?
B: It's behind the supermarket which is near the cinema.

Track 29

Sophie: Hi, Jane. How are you settling in to life at university?
Jane: Fine, except I don't really know what there is to do in town. I haven't had time to look around yet. You've been here for a year – could you give me some ideas?
Sophie: Of course! There's lots of places for students. Firstly, if you go across the bridge over the river outside the campus and turn left … Oh no, sorry, that's the garage … turn right, then you'll get to the bowling alley, which is really popular at the weekends because it's so close to the campus. On Friday nights they have a special discount for students.
Jane: Oh, that's great! I love bowling.
Sophie: So, … do you like sports, Jane?
Jane: Yes, I go running and swimming, and I play badminton.
Sophie: In that case, there's a running track behind the university campus and I think they have a badminton court at the sports centre.
Jane: Actually, I'm happy just to run in the park.
Sophie: Well, there's a large park in town, too. If you go down the road opposite the bowling alley and take the first right, then you'll get to the park. It's quite big and there's a lake in it. You can take a boat out on it. The university rowing team practise there.
Jane: What about places to eat out? Are there any good student hang-outs?
Sophie: Absolutely. There's the Elm Tree Café, which is down the road from the post office in the opposite direction from the river. The café is on a fork in the main road and it's quite an institution round here.
Jane: OK, well, I'll have to check it out. I'm looking for a part-time job so maybe I'll be able to find work there.
Sophie: Mm, you should try – they're always looking for new staff and they often hire students. Now have I forgotten any other important places? Oh yes, you like sport, so I should mention the leisure centre. Don't get it confused with the swimming baths, which are down the road from the supermarket. The leisure centre is opposite. There aren't any swimming baths there, but you can get a student leisure card which will let you into both. So, you see, there is quite a lot to do in this town.
Jane: It seems like there is. Well, thanks for all the information, Sophie.
Sophie: No problem. See you soon.

Track 30

1   78A High Trees Street, Sydney, 2316
2   354 Castle Avenue, Edinburgh, E5 7HU
3   86 The Drive, New York, 45008

Track 31

Administrator: Hello, have you come to enrol for your course or pay your fees?
Student: Um, both actually.
Administrator: OK, that's fine. You can enrol here with me, and then go to the next desk for fee payment. So, first of all can I have your name?
Student: Yes, it's Peter Taylor. That's Taylor with a Y.

Administrator:	So, it's T–A–Y–L–O–R.
Student:	That's right. Do you need my middle name?
Administrator:	No, just your first and last names, thanks. And what course are you doing?
Student:	I'm taking a BSc in Economics.
Administrator:	OK, that's in the Faculty of Mathematics.
Student:	Oh! I thought it was in the Faculty of Business and Management.
Administrator:	It was last year, but the course has moved to the Mathematics faculty this year.
Student:	Oh, thanks for letting me know.
Administrator:	No problem. Now where are you going to be living – on campus, or in private accommodation?
Student:	University accommodation. I'm in room 112 Ashley Residence.
Administrator:	Did you say Ashley Residence, the one in Duke Street? It's just that there's another residence called Askey Residence so it's confusing sometimes. I don't want to make a mistake on the computer records, otherwise you won't receive any university mail.
Student:	It's definitely Ashley: A–S–H–L–E–Y.
Administrator:	Great. And what about your home address – on our records it says 56 Grove Street, Manchester, M1 9JA. Is that correct?
Student:	Actually there's a small mistake, it's M4 not M1. The rest is correct, 9JA.
Administrator:	OK, I think that's all. You're enrolled on your course so you can go and pay your fees now.
Student:	Thanks. Bye.

Track 32

Students' Union assistant:	Hi, there. Can I help you?
Student:	Yes, I'd like to find out more information about the services here at the Students' Union.
SUA:	Of course, we're here to help you throughout your time at university.
Student:	So, what kind of help can you give me, exactly?
SUA:	Well, our job focuses on three main areas: giving advice and information to students, arranging social events and campaigning for students' rights.
Student:	Right. And what about help with things relating to everyday life?
SUA:	Well, we have a team of six advisors who work part-time and have expertise in certain areas including accommodation and travel.
Student:	Oh, that's great. And how can I contact the advisors?
SUA:	Right, there are several ways – you can come in to this office and speak to an advisor in person, or email us if you can't come in. And there's also a twenty-four-hour helpline. You can find the helpline number on your student card and you can call us at any time of day or night with any questions or worries you have.
Student:	OK, and thanks for your help.
SUA:	You're welcome.

Track 33

Library assistant:	Hi. How can I help you?
Student:	I'd like to register to use the library, please.
LA:	OK, that's fine. Now can I have some details from you? What's your name and student ID number?
Student:	Simon Anderson, that's A–N–D–E–R–S–O–N.
LA:	And ID number?
Student:	Er ... Hold on ... Let me look ... it's AND105763.
LA:	AND105769.
Student:	No, it's AND105763.
LA:	Thank you. And what course are you studying, Simon?
Student:	Geography.
LA:	Is that in the Faculty of Environmental Science or Earth Science?
Student:	It's in the Earth Science faculty.
LA:	Right. Now, are you living in university halls of residence?

Student:	No, I'm in private accommodation – do you need my address?
LA:	Yes, please.
Student:	It's Flat 3, 24 Lavender Gardens, London, SW12 3AG.
LA:	Can you spell the street name for me?
Student:	Yes, it's L–A–V–E–N–D–E–R Gardens.
LA:	And do you have a contact telephone number?
Student:	Is my mobile number OK?
LA:	Yes, that's fine.
Student:	Just let me find my phone. Right the number is 07988 566341 (079, double 8, 5, double 6, 341).
LA:	Let me just check that – 07988 566341. So, Simon did you have a tour of the library facilities during your induction?
Student:	Unfortunately, I missed it – could you give me a quick tour now?

Track 34

Library assistant:	I can't give you a tour now, I'm afraid. I have to stay here at the Help Desk but I can show you places on this map of the library.
Student:	That would be helpful, thanks.
LA:	OK, so we're here at the Help Desk, next to the Service Desk, where you go to borrow and return books. The maximum number of books you can borrow at any one time is ten.
Student:	Yes, I see.
LA:	Opposite the Service Desk is the Training Room, which is used by library staff to give demonstrations of the computer systems to staff and students. But the entrance is round the other side.
Student:	Is the Training Room beside the Quiet Room?
LA:	Yes, that's right, with the entrance round the front too. It's important to remember that all mobile phones must be switched off in this room.
Student:	Of course. And what about books – where can I find the books for my course?
LA:	Good question. You're studying Geography so, if you walk past the Service Desk, turn right, no sorry turn left, and continue on past the Philosophy section, you'll find the Geography section. The copying facilities are on the left. Now one more important thing is the Group Study Room and the booking system. If you're working on a project with other students and you want to discuss things with each other, you can go to the room in the corner at the opposite end of the library from the copiers. That's the Group Study Room. It's between the Sociology section and the TV room. The Group Study Room must be booked forty-eight hours in advance.
Student:	Right, thanks. Can I keep this map?
LA:	Actually, this is the last one I have, but I can make a copy for you.
Student:	That would be great, thanks.
LA:	Oh, I should also explain how you book the Group Study Room.
Student:	Oh, yes, so how do I do that?
LA:	You can only book this room using the online reservation system. The same one you use to reserve books that are currently on loan.
Student:	I thought it was called the online catalogue system.
LA:	No, that's for searching for things in the library; the reservation system is what you use to make a room booking.
Student:	And can I access that from outside the library?
LA:	Yes, via the library website. You will need to enter the name and student number of each student in the group too, so make sure you have these to hand when you make the booking. But all this is explained on the home page of the website. Once you've made your reservation request, you'll receive a confirmation email from the library to say whether your booking has been successful or not. If not, you can try to arrange another time.
Student:	Well that sounds fairly easy.
LA:	Yes, you'll be fine. It's all quite straightforward really.
Student:	Thanks.

Track 35

Tour guide: Now, not only do we have lots of historical architecture here in the town of Tanbridge, we also have a rich variety of famous residents. Of course, everyone has heard of the famous writers Jim Harman, Anna Collins and Ian Cheriton, or I. H. Cheriton, as he is better known. And they have all lived in our small town! In fact, Anna Collins, the celebrated romance novelist, spent all her life in this town. She lived by the town square, where there is a plaque to commemorate her. She died in 1968 and you can see her gravestone in Tanbridge Cemetery. You may know Anna from her most famous work, *The Pride of Angels*, which won numerous awards and for which she was a runner-up for the Herald Prize in 1950.

James Harman also lived here between 1975 and 1990. A bestselling horror writer, he got many of his themes for his haunting novels from this very town. He passed away a year after leaving Tanbridge and although he isn't buried in the town, we do have a statue of him on the roundabout as you enter the town.

Now, I. H. Cheriton has been the Poet Laureate for three years and he lives in Tanbridge today. His home is the red house by the river. Not only a poet, he has also written ten novels that have topped the book sales charts. He always does a lot of work for local charities and is quite a gem in this town.

Lastly, another famous resident of Tanbridge is Sylvia Daniels. She grew up in Tanbridge and went to the local comprehensive here. You can see her childhood home just across the river by the post office. Now I am sure you all know her for her latest film *Planet Dust*, which has just reached number one at the cinema box office. But she wasn't always an actress. Before she headed for Hollywood, you could have seen her waiting tables in The Dorage Restaurant here in town! She often comes back to visit as her family all still live here. If you're lucky, you may even catch a glimpse of her!

Track 36

Reviewer: Welcome to the latest episode of *Film Finest* with me, Liz O'Donnell. The films I'll be reviewing in this episode are *What Happens in the Night*, the new horror film by acclaimed director Jan de Neiburg, and *Happy as Larry*, a new romance comedy starring Harrison Wyatt and Sonya Smith. Let's start with *What Happens in the Night*. Set in a convent school in the 1950s, this film tells the story of two boys who are haunted by apparitions of monks. The film has the feel of a comic book as it's shot in black and white with occasional shots of vivid colour. De Neiburg, the director, said he wanted some elements to stand out and he has used colour to do it. I would say quite effectively. He claims his inspiration for the film is his own experiences growing up in 1950s Liverpool. A believer in ghosts himself, he thought he saw ghosts in his school years. Ghosts or not, this film is certainly haunting. *What Happens in the Night* is a film that will scare you. I wouldn't say it's the best horror film to come out this year, but it's certainly shot beautifully, and it's not hard to follow. So, unlike some recent horror films, you don't have to sit in dedicated concentration for two hours trying to keep up with a complex plot! An enjoyable film, I would give it four stars.

In *Happy as Larry*, Sonya Smith and Harrison Wyatt play two people who fall in love but cannot be together because of their families. The build-up to the film has certainly been epic, with gossip about both co-stars in the papers. Rumour has it that Smith and Wyatt aren't the best of friends. In fact, on the set they barely spoke to each other! I have to say, though, this doesn't come across in the film and they look like a great couple. *Happy as Larry* is a move away from the usual films Sonya makes – she is better known for her roles in action films – but she has shown herself to be a capable comedy actress. However, I'm not sure this is the finest film to do it in. Both men and women alike can get something from this film, but the romance angle is overplayed and the laughs are few and far between. If you want romance, this film is fine, but if you want comedy, I would recommend seeing something else. I would give it three stars.

Now, there are some new video releases which are going to be coming out ...

Track 37

Interviewer: So, we have Phyllis Bailey here to talk to us about fame. Her new book, *Famous for Fifteen Minutes* is coming out on Monday. So Phyllis, welcome. What do you think fame means to us these days?

Phyllis: Well, <u>famous people are everywhere and although we know nearly all there is to know about these people – their lives are splashed all over magazines and television – they've retained their mystery.</u> The public are always eager to find out more about them and this fuels the paparazzi to photograph them. <u>It's true that there are more celebrities around than ever before</u>, but the number of really important famous people probably hasn't changed greatly. <u>This is because people became famous for only a short time.</u> Andy Warhol once famously said, 'In the future, everyone will be famous for fifteen minutes', and I think there's some truth in that. <u>One day a person is famous and the next they are forgotten.</u> Take, for example, contestants on reality television shows. After maybe six months we never see them again. This also highlights another characteristic of fame: in the past people became famous because of something they had done, or because of their talent. Nowadays these things aren't necessary. I personally think this is a great pity.

Interviewer: Is fame particularly beneficial now?

Phyllis: Well let's look at the winners and losers when it comes to fame. Many people think that celebrities are the losers in this new media world, but that isn't necessarily the case. Take, for example, actors and actresses. They often complain about a lack of privacy, but privacy is possible. There are many celebrities who aren't constantly in the papers. Much as they complain, they chase the publicity and then blame it on the media. <u>In fact, the paparazzi, who photograph the rich and famous, are often seen as figures of hate for this. They come off much worse in the end, because they are so disliked by the public and celebrities.</u> But in reality, they are making the celebrities and their managers even richer. In fact, because of the cult of fame nowadays, we can see media executives making even more money and celebrities signing multi-million pound deals. <u>And who pays for this? Well, all of us. Cinema and concert ticket prices have risen and DVDs cost more than ever.</u> Merchandising makes a fortune for the famous these days. And although we are paying for it, <u>the rewards go to only a small elite – the big players, the stars and the executives, but they miss a lot of the creative talent in the industry, like the people who write the screenplays. They are still on the same salary they were on ten years ago.</u> Executives certainly have a difficult job managing their clients, but they get rewarded well for doing so. I for one think these rewards should be more fairly spread.

Interviewer: How could this be done? Are you ...?

Track 38

Guide: Thank you for coming along to the Cultural Sydney talk. I'm going to start by telling you about the Yellow Plaque scheme, which has been running in Sydney for over forty years and has been incredibly successful. When you are walking around the city, you'll see some buildings with a small round yellow plaque on them. If you take a closer look, you'll see the name and details of a famous person who lived in that very place. We have, at present, 130 plaques up in the city. <u>The scheme has been great for tourism, but it was really started to raise awareness of the rich history of Sydney, both locally and nationally, and we think we've managed to do this. We also wanted to make people aware of the impressive list of important people who have lived in this city, and we've certainly achieved that.</u> But that's not all. Although not part of our original aims, the scheme has also helped preserve some of the older and more important buildings in Sydney because people now know that these buildings are a link to our past; some of the buildings are actually over 180 years old, which, for Australia, is ancient! <u>We actually think that this is where the scheme has achieved the most success; in raising the profile of our rich history.</u> Of course, it has helped tourism, but not only that, locals also walk around looking at the plaques. <u>It has been really wonderful in highlighting our past.</u> Some people are quite surprised to see who has lived here; take Errol Flynn for example. He was married in Sydney.

We are planning on putting more plaques up and a common question is how can people nominate a figure to be put on a plaque. It's quite a simple process. Applications can be downloaded from our website. <u>If you want to nominate someone for a plaque you just need the person's name, where they lived and you need three signatures to approve your application.</u> Our panel then checks that all the data you've submitted is correct and hopefully, within a year a new plaque will be erected. But you can't nominate just anyone! <u>A plaque can only be given to a person who is famous and has achieved something out of the ordinary, like an important politician or world-record breaking sportsman, for example.</u> We aim to have fifty new plaques up within the next three years, and we have plenty of funding to do so. Our funding comes from three sources: the local council, community donations and the tourist board. Whereas in the past the tourist board put in the majority of funding, now public donations count for sixty-five per cent of all total funds! In fact, our funding is so healthy now; there are plans to expand the scheme.

Track 39

Guide: At the moment, we only have yellow plaques for all the famous people, but we are aiming to produce different coloured plaques so that people can do specific walks. For example, if they are interested in famous sports personalities they can do a tour following the red plaques – the colour we are aiming to use for these people. We are looking at introducing grey, white and green plaques as well. We are thinking of using grey plaques to signify people who have done important work within the government and white plaques for those who have done good works in the community. Lastly, our green plaques we think will be very popular, these will be for painters and sculptors, leaving our yellow ones for writers, actors and other people of note. We do hope you enjoy looking at the plaques around the city. We have guide books on sale in the gift shop where you can find all the plaques. These are priced at $11.99.

CD 2

Track 01

Tutor: Hi, James. How's your alternative energy research project going?

James: To be honest, I'm a bit confused about how to do the research for all the different energy types.

Tutor: Well, the first thing you do is to make sure you focus your question, otherwise you'll have too much to read and you won't be able to select the key arguments.

James: So how do I do that?

Tutor: Start with the general topic of alternative energy and then keep asking questions until you've narrowed the topic down to one particular area. Then, when you have your question, make a list of the reading you will need. This list should be general to give you some background, but remember you'll need to focus on the issues related to the question, so the reading list should also be specific to the actual energy source you've chosen, whether it's wind or solar or wave power.

James: And then start reading?

Tutor: Absolutely. You need to start straight away, but don't forget to make notes as you read, otherwise you won't be able to keep track of ideas for future reference purposes.

James: Yes, that makes sense. I think that's my main problem – I don't recall where I've read different ideas so I can't find them again later. And my friends have warned me that not recording ideas in a system can really hinder your progress.

Tutor: Your friends are right – it's a common problem amongst students. You need a system. Anyway, once you've done the reading and made all your notes, you need to organise them so that you can analyse and think about what you've read.

James: But I prefer to just start writing and then go back and look at my notes later.

Tutor: Hmm ... I wouldn't recommend it. I think you need to give yourself more time to digest the material and arrange it into some kind of system ready for analysis in terms of relevance to your research question.

James: Well, that's a great help. Thank you, Professor Jenkins.

Tutor: You're welcome. Come and see me again if you have any more problems.

Track 02

John: Hi, Mary. How are you?

Mary: I'm fine, thanks, John. How's your essay going?

John: Not so good, actually. Would you be able to help me with it?

Mary: Of course. What do you want to know?

John: Well, just the type of information you're going to write about. I won't copy you – I just want some ideas to get me started.

Mary: Well, Mr Jones advised us to focus on just two or three forms of non-traditional energy for our evaluation so I think I'm going to choose solar – it's fairly easy to evaluate.

John: Are you going to explain both the positive and negative aspects?

Mary:	Well, Mr Jones warned us not to get too involved in the ethical aspects of the topic. So I'm going to structure my essay by using the advantages and disadvantages of each energy form. That's why I also want to talk about biofuels – I think there are more disadvantages.
John:	Oh, I see what you're doing – using the negative points of one to highlight the positive points of the other! That's a smart idea. And what about the third energy source?
Mary:	Mm, I was having difficulty choosing between nuclear and wind because they're both problematic but I've decided to do nuclear for my presentation instead.
John:	Thanks, Mary. Chatting to you has helped me think a bit more clearly about my essay.
Mary:	That's fine. Good luck with it.

Track 03

Shirley:	Hi there, guys. Nice to see you.
Tom:	And you. So, are we going to finalise what we're doing for the Environmental Science presentation today?
Chris:	I hope so. The presentation is next week.
Shirley:	Actually, I wanted to talk to you about this because I think we need to take out some of the information we're including.
Chris:	Oh, really? Like what, Shirley?
Shirley:	Well, I'd like to suggest taking out the background details – I think it's just too much information to fit into ten minutes.
Tom:	But isn't it important to make sure the audience understands the context?
Shirley:	I don't think so, and anyway, we could include the background details on the handout.
Tom:	OK, I'm with you on that. Chris, what do you think?
Chris:	Yes, OK, that's fine. I'll add the details to the handout. Anything else?
Shirley:	Yes. I'm not sure whether the solar energy statistics will be too much for the audience to take in – there's a lot of numbers and graphs. Can we put the statistics on a handout too?
Chris:	Mm, I see your point. We don't want people looking at lots of numbers while we're speaking.
Tom:	But without the statistics, I don't see how we can support our main ideas.
Shirley:	Actually, you're right, Tom. I hadn't thought about that. In that case, can we delete the diagrams? It's going to take too much time to explain them.
Tom:	Hm. Let's think about that a bit more. If we have to choose between taking out the statistics or the diagrams, I think we should opt for the diagrams – they're less crucial to the presentation. What do you both think?
Shirley:	I think it's going to work much better than the original plan we had.
Chris:	Absolutely. We won't have to worry about talking for longer than fifteen minutes if we remove the diagrams and focus on the main ideas and statistics. Shall we all meet again tomorrow to finalise the details?

Track 04

Hannah:	Hi, everyone! Sorry I'm late.
Louise:	Don't worry, Hannah, we've only just started. We thought we should go over the theories we've studied so far so we're ready for the seminar discussion on Thursday afternoon.
Hannah:	Of course, you're right. I don't think I can remember all the theories related to consumer energy consumption.
Mike:	No, Hannah. That's the reading for Friday's lecture. Thursdays' seminar discussion is about the current thinking on alternative energy.
Hannah:	Oh, yes. Sorry. I'm a bit disorganised at the moment.
Louise:	Never mind. So, Mike, what do think about the academics' point of view on nuclear energy?
Mike:	Well, I think I have to agree with them on price being a factor for choosing nuclear in the long term.
Louise:	Me too. It's definitely the most cost effective measure. Don't you agree, Hannah?
Hannah:	To start with I didn't, but the text Professor Edwards gave us persuaded me. The only thing that concerns me is that there have been some disasters in various parts of the world.
Louise:	Yes, some texts warn of the dangers of nuclear power using previous disasters as examples.
Mike:	I know what you mean, but I suppose the risk is minimal these days. What do you think about wind and solar energy in terms of the price in relation to the advantages? For me, they're just not worth it – both are expensive and it's difficult to predict the amount of energy each one will produce.

Hannah:	You know, Mike, I'm afraid I don't share your opinion. This text here talks about the likelihood of improved technology increasing the amount of energy and reducing the costs in the future.
Louise:	Yes, but that's not enough proof to be sure of the relationship between the costs and the benefits.
Mike:	Exactly, the evidence seems incomplete to me.
Hannah:	Well, that's something we can follow up on with the rest of the group in the seminar on Thursday.

Track 05

Tutor:	Good morning, Phil, Jackie. I hope your project is going well.
Phil:	Morning, Mr Jackson.
Jackie:	Hi Mr Jackson. Well, we've made a start on analysing the different forms of renewable energy, but unfortunately we don't really agree on some points.
Tutor:	OK, why don't we talk about it?
Phil:	Well, Jackie believes that all forms of renewable energy are beneficial economically, whereas I doubt that that's true for all of them.
Tutor:	Such as?
Phil:	Such as wind, wave and solar energy because they're less reliable.
Tutor:	That's a valid point but I don't think that's a large enough factor to disregard it completely.
Jackie:	Exactly, that's what I said.
Phil:	However, another drawback is that they're generally very expensive to produce.
Tutor:	Yes, you're right. And that *is* a concern when evaluating their usefulness in future.
Jackie:	I agree with you to a point, but it's likely that the cost will come down. I read a report in the *Journal of Environmental Science* that estimates the cost would fall by twenty per cent over the next ten years, which is significant, isn't it?
Tutor:	Absolutely, Jackie. But you need to think about how difficult it is to predict the future cost of non-traditional energy sources before you believe the report. Remember: in your project I want to see evidence of critical analysis. Make sure you've analysed all the information rather than just accepting the information that you agree with. Also it's very important that you demonstrate wide reading around the subject.
Jackie:	I know, it's just that I'm not convinced that it's going to continue to be that expensive, especially if there's a demand from consumers.
Phil:	Well, what about if we analyse the costing process as part of our project?
Tutor:	That's an excellent idea, Phil. OK, so let's imagine that we want to forecast the cost of producing solar energy. How could we do that, Jackie?
Jackie:	Um, well, I think we'd have to start by working out how many hours of daylight there are in the UK per year.
Phil:	The Meteorological Office would have data on that.
Jackie:	Then estimate the number of hours of sun to get a rough total.
Phil:	And then I suppose we'd need to work out how much it would cost to supply the average home with solar power, and then extrapolate *that* to get a number for the whole country.
Tutor:	Good, and don't forget the price of power conversion stations – this will have a significant impact on overall expenditure. And there's one more factor you haven't taken into account yet, regarding the consumers.
Jackie:	Um ... whether they would change from traditional to renewable energy?
Tutor:	No, but think about what might make them change?
Jackie:	Oh, yes. How much they would be willing to pay.
Tutor:	Exactly. Well done.

Track 06

Phil:	So, our project is going to cover three main areas. Firstly, comparing the main forms of alternative energy: solar, wind, wave, and bio fuels in terms of production costs. Secondly, we'll take solar energy as an example and do a cost prediction, and lastly we'll analyse whether they're likely to replace traditional fossil fuels in the future.
Tutor:	That sounds like a comprehensive project with a good focus. Now, what data are you going to use and what approach will you use for the analysis?

Jackie: Ah! Now that's something we *do* agree on! We want to use the reports you gave us in our last lecture and some statistics from the government Environment and Energy Department. In terms of analysis, we're going to use a cross-referencing method where we compare each of the government reports with the Robertson report and highlight any differences. Then we'll analyse these to see why the differences exist and where more research needs to be done.

Track 07

Lecturer: OK, so to finish I want to look at the resources available for researching UK census information for the essay you'll be writing at the end of this module. There are many resources for the study of the civilian population and family history out there ranging from public to academic to commercial. Some are available for the public to access free of charge, whilst others are only available by payment of fees, or restricted to academics and subject to registration. Some are more appropriate to family or genealogical investigation, others to historical population research.

So if we start at the beginning of the list on your handout, you'll see firstly there is the Family Records Centre based in central London. The centre and their website are available to anyone in the country who has an interest in researching demographic data. Their work might be useful to give you an overview of the general sorts of data and services available. Unfortunately, you do have to pay a registration charge of £20 for a year's access to their material.

The next resource on the list is Genes Reunited, which is mainly for people who want to find out more about their ancestors. There are some good interactive tools on this website, especially the one which shows you how to manipulate the National Census Association's statistical data. Although Genes Reunited is very useful, it is used by a range of businesses and therefore accessing the site will cost you.

Now, the third item on the handout is The National Census Association, which contains the most up-to-date data as it's compiled from official government census data every ten years. Both companies and individuals are able to access all their resources without payment, so this may be a good place to start your research.

Finally, I'd just like to draw your attention to two journals at the bottom of the handout. The first one, *Journal of Historical Migration*, is not actually a journal but a collection of articles on a website. Anyway, you might like to take a look at it because it has several articles on the importance of recording census data from a historical research perspective. This site is available to the general public so you don't have to pay or register. The other one, the *Journal of Social Demography*, is only available using your university online journals login details as it can only be accessed by those studying or researching in higher education. Right. Well, that should be enough reading for you.

Track 08

Lecturer: Today I'd like to continue from last week's lecture by looking at what helps people successfully integrate into a new culture. Whereas the reasons for migration are nowadays fairly easy to identify and largely related to employment opportunities or political instability, the factors behind being able to adapt to the new culture and create a new life are considerably more complex. Let's start with an overview of the issues as shown on this diagram. Starting on the left of the diagram there are two lists of factors: internal and external. It's important to notice that the internal factors, in other words those based on an individual's personality, are divided into positive factors – trusting others and acknowledging that people are different, and negative – being afraid and being suspicious of people. You might think that the list of negative factors would include discrimination, but it doesn't because discrimination comes under the larger category of fear. Now, what you should also notice is that the external factors are not labelled in this way. It's much more difficult to know how to measure the affects of external factors and whether they actually are external or not. The influence of family relationships, climate, beliefs and values, and the ability to communicate in the language of the new culture have wide ranging effects which are difficult to measure and can distort any research.

Now focus on the centre of the diagram, and you'll see this phrase: 'Coping strategies'. This is important because studies have shown that people who integrate well into a new culture, and that is *any* culture by the way, are those who have eradicated any negativity, and made positive choices, and adopted coping strategies such as observing people, and taking time to listen and ask questions in order to diminish the effects of culture shock. What we have observed is that people who demonstrate positive coping strategies such as observing, listening, and questioning end up by understanding the host culture better and integrating quicker and more successfully. However, those who choose to be critical of the differences, and therefore react negatively to the host culture, are likely to have increased feelings of alienation. This alienation can tail off and become the beginning of acceptance if a person has some positive experiences, but it usually deteriorates quickly into isolation.

Track 09

Lecturer: Many people have immigrated to Britain and become citizens over the last 200 years, and in today's lecture I'd like to look at the various laws or acts of parliament introduced to deal with those people who came to live in Britain. In 1793 there was the Aliens Act, which the British government introduced to control the number of refugees fleeing to Britain to escape the Revolution in France. Compared to today, when refugees have to complete a long and complicated application process before arrival, in 1793 all that was required by the authorities was that individuals had to register at the port where they arrived. The collection of personal information started in 1844 with the Naturalisation Act, which was updated in 1870. The main difference in the 1870 Act was that applicants who wanted to stay in Britain had to have served the Crown or to have lived in the country for at least five years before being considered. Both these acts allowed the government to control the number of people coming into the country. These changes were fairly insignificant regarding people's freedoms and the amount of state intervention involved. However, in the twentieth century this began to change. The Alien Registration Act was introduced in 1914 and when the First World War broke out, all aliens over the age of sixteen had to register at local police stations, be of 'good character' and demonstrate a working knowledge of English. The reason for this act was to create a feeling of patriotism among migrant communities and also to stop spies from Europe infiltrating the country.

And after the Second World War, the meaning of British nationality was re-defined again, this time to encourage residents from British colonies to come to Britain to help rebuild the country. This was the British Nationality Act of 1948. The condition was that potential migrants had to demonstrate that they wanted to work and were fit and healthy. Finally, there was the Commonwealth Immigration Act of 1962. Legislation was passed to restrict the number of Commonwealth immigrants to Britain. Although many people still wanted to come to Britain to obtain good jobs, the Act now meant applicants had to get work permits, which were given mostly to skilled immigrants, such as doctors.

In the next session I want to look at more contemporary acts, for instance ...

Track 10

Lecturer: This morning I'd like to focus on New York as a model for understanding immigration patterns in relation to *national* rather than *international* change. Firstly, it is important to understand that migration patterns are primarily affected by the rules of immigration which determine the conditions of entry. After that, internal changes can affect patterns considerably. To highlight my first point let's study this diagram of Ellis Island and the process of admitting immigrants in the late nineteenth and early twentieth centuries. Upon arrival at Ellis Island, people underwent a series of examinations and questions before being allowed to enter the US. First of all, there was a medical inspection to ensure the immigrants were not bringing in any contagious diseases. Anyone who did not pass the medical examination was refused entry to New York and sent home on the next available ship. If the examination was passed, immigrants were required to take a further examination; this time a legal examination to establish whether they had any criminal convictions. After this, immigrants were able to change currency and purchase tickets for onward rail travel from New York. Having completed this simple process, immigrants were told to wait – this wait could be as long as five hours – before boarding a ferry to take them to New York City. This simple system allowed millions of immigrants to enter the US and is largely responsible for the ethnic make-up of the city today. Even though the immigrants themselves may have had a variety of reasons for deciding to migrate, it was only possible because of US national immigration laws.

Moving on to the second point – how changes *within* a country can have as much or more of an effect than those *outside* the country. Various parts of New York have changed radically in their ethnic make-up over the last 200 years: communities became wealthier, governments introduced new laws, and employment opportunities came and went. These factors affect where people choose to live or force them to move to somewhere different. For example, most people think that the population has changed in Manhattan due to the rise of its importance as a financial trade centre, which is true to some extent. But like the Ellis Island example, a change in politics, namely a change of mayor, allowed the city to boom as a financial centre, and this resulted in different types of people moving to the area. Brooklyn is an interesting example, too and we'll be looking at it as our case study later in the lecture. Whereas it used to be a predominantly working class area of the city and therefore attracted unskilled migrant workers, nowadays its fame as a centre for up-and-coming artists and musicians means it has attracted a new and much more diverse population of middle class residents. Finally, Queens has shown a dramatic change in its population over the last fifty years due to the airports there. This means that the number of airline staff living in the area has dramatically increased and changed the nature of the local population.

Finally, I'd like to use Brooklyn as a case study of local change. Brooklyn's population has changed significantly over the years and this can most easily be seen in its economic activity. Tracing the Brooklyn industries back from the current financial services companies, to manufacturing in the 1950s, to shipbuilding in the 1900s, we can map this onto average wages and therefore the type and class of resident. And this has affected the population density too which has been steadily increasing over the past 100 years from 1.5 million in 1900, through to 2 million in the middle of the twentieth century, to the 2.3 million inhabitants today. In fact Brooklyn is suffering from considerable overpopulation now. But this large population increase was due not to employment but the building of the subway which linked Brooklyn to other areas of New York. Prior to this at the beginning of the twentieth century the only way of transportation was the Brooklyn Bridge. Another factor which traditionally increases the desire for the middle classes to live in a particular place is the extent and type of local heritage, especially for those people with young children. In Brooklyn this is evident in the increase in population after the construction of Coney Island. The modern day equivalent of this is the restoration of Prospect Park, which has brought more middle income families into the area.

Track 11

Anna:	Excuse me. Where I can fill up my water bottle?
John:	There's a water cooler just inside the main doors. Is this your first time here?
Anna:	Yes, I just had my induction last week. I'm Anna.
John:	Hi! I'm John. If you have any problems and I'm around, please just ask.
Anna:	Have you been coming here long?
John:	Yes. I've lived here all my life, just a couple of miles away. I started coming here when I was just a kid. I suppose I'm quite a faithful member. My brother and father come here too!
Anna:	Wow! That's impressive!
John:	Thanks. I enjoy it so much because it basically gives me so much energy for the day. It's unusual that I'm here at this time. I work pretty hard and so I try to fit it in before work usually. I start work at seven, so I usually get in here by about five thirty.
Anna:	Uh, it must still be dark at that time?
John:	Yes, it is!
Anna:	That must take some willpower!
John:	It does but it's worth it. You should try an early session; it really makes you feel good about the day! How often are you planning on coming?
Anna:	I was thinking maybe just twice a week at the beginning and then build up from there. What do you think?
John:	That's a good idea! When are you thinking of coming?
Anna:	Probably evenings. Is it generally very busy then?
John:	It can be. I came in the evening yesterday and it was quite busy. In fact, a funny thing happened. I was on the treadmill and suddenly water started hitting me! It was the fire alarm! The sprinklers had gone off. I was absolutely soaked! It was the first time anything like that has happened, but it was pretty funny! Fortunately, it was a false alarm!
Anna:	Ha ha! So much excitement at the gym. I think I'm going to enjoy this!

Track 12

Salesman: Thank you for taking the time to see me today, Mr Jones. I'd just like to take a minute to outline our new step machines.

Mr Jones: No problem, I'm interested in getting a few. We don't have any in the gym yet.

Salesman: That's great. Well, let me talk you through the build of the step machine. If you have a look at the sales brochure you can see what they look like on page 14.

Mr Jones: OK.

Salesman: These machines are two metres tall, so they tend to stand out. The tallest part is the holding frame. At the top there we have the main grips. These grips, when they are held, monitor heart rate so that the user can check they are working out at their optimum heart rate.

Mr Jones: That's great. And where does this rate show up?

Salesman: They'll be able to see it on the screen below. This screen is fully digital and shows not only their heart rate, but the number of steps they've taken and the distance they've travelled. On the panel there they also have a selection of workouts. They can set it by distance, or time, or by the amount of calories they want to burn. They can even set it to climb a famous mountain or hill, or walk up the Leaning Tower of Pisa for example!

Mr Jones: That's great, I like those more fun settings.

Salesman: And the great thing is you can have people climbing up Mount Everest, for example, every day for ten years and this machine will still be in perfect working order. It's made to last. It not only has a metallic spine but durable pedals made from the most high-tech materials on the market.

Mr Jones: And the machine works via a wheel in the centre? That's unusual, isn't it?

Salesman: Yes, it is, but we find a central wheel lasts much longer than a pump system. The central wheel is attached to a bracket which ensures each step movement is as smooth as the last. The final feature I should point out to you is the side supports, which ensure safety for all machine users. If users feel tired, they can hold on to these and slow down their stepping!

Mr Jones: I see! Well, I think I might take three of them.

Track 13

Receptionist: OK, Alice, I just need a few more details to start your membership. Your full name is Alice Wilson yes?

Alice: No, Watson.

Receptionist: Oh yes! I'm sorry. Which age range are you?

Alice: Well, I'm just out of the 16–25 bracket! I'm 26 now.

Receptionist: Great, 26–35.

Alice: Yes.

Receptionist: And do you have any health problems which may affect your exercise?

Alice: No, I don't have any health conditions.

Receptionist: I'll put none. Do you do any exercise at the moment?

Alice: Not much. I exercise a couple of times a week.

Receptionist: And what do you do?

Alice: Well, I used to play tennis, but I stopped. Now I only go swimming.

Receptionist: OK ... And why have you decided to join up?

Alice: Just to improve my fitness. I don't want to lose any weight or build muscles or anything!

Receptionist: Fine. Well, I would recommend doing the Level 2 workout programme to begin with. It takes about forty minutes to do the whole programme. I'll get you an information sheet so you can see what it involves.

Track 14

Debbie: Hi, Penny. How are you doing? Have you just been to the gym?

Penny: Hi, Debbie. I'm good, thanks. Yes, I've just finished a workout. How are you?

Debbie: Yes, good. I'm planning on going to the gym later but it's hard finding the time now I've got a child!

Penny: I bet it is! Have you tried any of their new exercise classes?

Debbie: Yes, I tried some last week. I wanted to go to yoga, but it was full up. I went to the dance class instead. It was really fun. Oh! And kickboxing last Thursday too. That was exhausting.

Penny:	Well, you didn't miss much at yoga. <u>I went there last Friday and it was far too hard. I couldn't do most of the exercises!</u>
Debbie:	Oh no! Are you going to try anything else?
Penny:	Well, I was thinking of trying the aerobics class.
Debbie:	My friend did that one, and said the instructor was awful.
Penny:	Well, I'll probably give it a miss then. <u>I've got to go to a conference next week</u> anyway, so I'll be away from Tuesday to Friday.
Debbie:	Oh, lucky you!

Track 15

Receptionist:	Hello, and welcome to Smith's Gym.
Brad:	Hi there. I'd like to become a member.
Receptionist:	Yes, of course. We just need to fill out a couple of forms, and then I can show you around the gym.
Brad:	That would be great.
Receptionist:	Let's start with the membership form. Can I have your name, please?
Brad:	Yes, sure. Brad Simmons.
Receptionist:	Is that Simmons with a 'd' or without?
Brad:	<u>Without. S–I–M–M–O–N–S.</u>
Receptionist:	Got it! And can I take a contact number, please?
Brad:	Yes, sure … <u>It's 0498355521 (0–4–9–8–3–treble 5–2–1).</u>
Receptionist:	OK … 0498355531.
Brad:	No, uh, it's 2–1 at the end.
Receptionist:	Great. And do you have an email address?
Brad:	Yes. Brad zero seven at elemnet dot com. That's e–l–e–m–n–e–t dot com.
Receptionist:	Right. Now, we've got three membership types here: bronze, which is just off peak and costs £21.00 a month; silver, which means you can use the gym at all times – this is £36.50. Or for just £5 more you can get a gold membership, which gives you free access to the squash and tennis courts and all classes.
Brad:	<u>For now I think I'll just take the silver.</u>
Receptionist:	That's fine, sir. That'll be £36.50 a month.
Brad:	Great. When can I start?
Receptionist:	Well, you'll need to have an induction first … We have spaces at two thirty, four forty-five, and eight fifteen tomorrow. Would any of these be suitable?
Brad:	I can't do tomorrow. Do you have anything for Saturday?
Receptionist:	<u>Is that the twelfth of November?</u>
Brad:	<u>No, it's the eleventh.</u>
Receptionist:	Yes …: Yes that's fine. Would two thirty be OK?
Brad:	That's fine.
Receptionist:	I'll book you in with our trainer Rob Ellis. Now, would you like me to show you around?
Brad:	That would be great.

Track 16

Receptionist:	OK, follow me. Let's go up the stairs to the main equipment room. … As you can see, we have all the treadmills, bikes and rowing machines in here. And the weights are in the corner.
Brad:	Great. And is that the pool over there? Can I use that with my membership?
Receptionist:	Yes, at any time. Just go through the glass doors on the left. As you can see, the pool is dominated by the diving board at the far end. It's impressively tall, and on the right hand side of the pool you can see we have two lanes. The first one is a slow lane for those who are trying to improve their fitness. It gets really busy! <u>The lane on the far right is what we call the club lane.</u> Because we reserve this for people who have membership, it is slightly less busy and the members can get a really good workout in it.
Brad:	That sounds great!
Receptionist:	Yes, it is good. <u>And then near us you can see a smaller area sectioned off nearly halfway across the pool. This area is where we put the school groups which come in the late afternoons during</u>

the week. Usually from about four. <u>We keep them confined to that space so that the other end can be used for free swimming</u>.

Brad:	<u>And what is the little round pool for?</u>
Receptionist:	<u>We call that the toddlers pool</u>. It's not very deep, and the mothers often bring their children in to teach them to swim in it.
Brad:	Great. Well, I am glad I can use the pool. It will be good to vary my exercise.
Receptionist:	Definitely. <u>When do you think you'll be coming?</u>
Brad:	<u>Most likely in the evenings. I'd like to come on Saturdays, but I often work then, so I think I'll have to miss that day and then come on Sundays.</u>
Receptionist:	Oh, so you'll be a regular visitor? That's great news! Can I ask why you chose Smith's Gym?
Brad:	<u>Well, actually the television advert prompted me to join</u>. It makes exercising look so much fun! I always thought going to the gym would be monotonous.
Receptionist:	No, not at all. It can be a lot of fun.
Brad:	<u>My aim is to reach my optimum fitness</u>. At the moment I think I'm a bit unhealthy, so I'd like to change that.
Receptionist:	Well, give it some time and I'm sure you will. Now, shall we go back and complete the payment details?

Track 17

See page 80 for text.

Track 18

Manager: Good morning, everyone. <u>I'd like to talk to you all about the department restructure and how it will affect our work. As you know, the company is expanding, and this means we'll need to recruit more staff and optimise our ways of working</u>. So I want to look at each of our teams and the changes which are planned to start next month. The Sales Team, headed by Gary Wilson, will be responsible for not only increasing the amount of business we do with our current customers but also searching out new clients. As this is likely to be a labour-intensive task, Gary's team will need more staff, which is where Linda French's Human Resources Team comes in. <u>Linda and Gary will collaborate on finding and employing twenty new sales members as soon as possible. However, not all staff will be recruited from outside. If this company is going to continue to thrive, each of the current team managers will need an assistant and these positions will be internal appointments.</u> Human Resources are sending out an email to all staff this week asking them if they would like to apply for one of the new positions, and interviews will begin next month.

Now, in order for the Sales Team to increase revenue, the <u>Research and Development Team have to come up with some innovative products which will be better than those offered by other companies</u>. Therefore, Zoe's team will start a month-long project to learn more about what our competitors make to help inform our design process. <u>Their target will be to design and create two new ranges of products this year</u>. As always, if any of you have an idea for a product, please contact Zoe about it; all ideas are welcome.

Lastly, but just as importantly, I'd like to talk about Ian Smith's team. <u>Obviously, after-care service is crucial to the expansion of the company,</u> so IT Support will be making sure that all our customers are called to discuss our service as part of the follow-up system. <u>Ian's team will also be upgrading our client support package to facilitate twenty-four-hour access, seven days a week</u>. Ian believes strongly that this will increase our competitiveness and be a real selling point for potential customers.

Track 19

Melanie: Welcome to this fire evacuation talk everyone. I'm Melanie Brookes, the fire safety manager here at Techbase, and my office is on the fourth floor if you ever need to find me.

Today I want to run through the fire evacuation procedure now that we're in a new building. First of all, can I just remind you that if you hear the fire alarm, you should always head towards the main stairs in order to leave the building. <u>Please assume that the alarm is real, except if it sounds at 11.00 a.m. on a Tuesday. At this time, it's always a test</u> – we hope. <u>It's vital that you do not spend time collecting your bags or personal belongings because this wastes valuable evacuation time.</u> When you have left the building, please look for the fire marshals, who will be wearing fluorescent orange jackets. They'll show you where the waiting area is, but just so you know, it's the park at the rear of the office block. Your department has a fire safety officer – I believe it's Susan Jenkins – and it's her job to make sure that everyone who signed in has vacated the building. <u>Susan will then tell the fire safety manager if there are any missing people</u>. Can I also remind you that you mustn't enter the building again until the fire safety manager, in other words, me, tells you that the situation is no longer dangerous.

Track 20

Marketing Manager:

Right team, this afternoon I want to go over the new marketing and advertising strategy so that everyone is clear on the streams for each of our product ranges.

<u>Let's start with toys for children</u>. Now, last year most of the advertising was done through leaflets posted through people's letterboxes across the city. However, the products are now selling well nationally in department stores rather than just in our local shop here in Leeds, so we're going to expand the budget and use print media. <u>By this I mean the national newspapers, in order to maximise the exposure to these products</u>. And despite the fact that our competitors advertise baby clothes on TV, we won't be using this method as our statistics show that it's just not cost-effective. <u>People don't pay much attention to TV ads for baby clothes, but we believe a picture in the newspapers will be much more attractive to potential customers. We're going with this method</u>.

<u>As far as clothing for expectant mothers is concerned, the campaign will move from newspapers to the internet due to the fact that we've seen an increase in internet shopping for clothes among women in general</u>.

And finally, baby food. Adverts for this are difficult to place, and we've previously tried ads in all three media. <u>Anyway, although our analysis has shown that the internet is one possibility, we're going to continue using television</u>; many other types of food are also advertised on TV and happy mothers and babies make a very strong image.

Track 21

Chief Executive Officer:

I'd like to start by welcoming everyone to our annual meeting and thanking you all for your hard work. It's been a great year for us in terms of expansion and optimising business opportunities, and I'm pleased to say that Benchmark Consulting is a thriving, successful company.

I'd like to take this opportunity to give you an overview of where the company began and where we'll be going in the next ten years. For those of you who've been with the company since the start, sorry if you already know all this, but we have so many new staff members that I thought it would be worth filling in some background information.

Benchmark Consulting was set up in 2000 by James Cox, a local entrepreneur who opened the first office in Melbourne. <u>His real achievement was to create a new consultancy system</u> which enabled clients to see which of the key areas of their business needed strengthening. James was incredibly successful with his system, and started the company off on a journey of expansion. He retired in 2006, and was succeeded by Fred Montgomery. <u>Fred shared James's views on consulting, and continued the expansion; he increased revenue to $5 million and opened a new office in Perth</u>. Soon the Benchmark Consulting system had become just that – the benchmark for many other consulting firms, and Fred took the opportunity to sell Benchmark for $10 million in 2008.

<u>Our new owners are, as you know, TFB Group Ltd., and their investment has allowed us to build our brand new headquarters here in Sydney</u>. TFB Group have brought us more exposure at a national level, and our most recent success has been winning a contract with the government of Australia, advising on management restructuring.

Now we ourselves have done a little reorganisation over the last year to maximise our productivity. We've thought long and hard about the best location for the Marketing Department as this is the key to facilitating our future business. <u>Although Perth has a large number of marketing companies, which enables us to learn from our competitors, it's Melbourne that's the gateway to international connections, and therefore we've decided to move all marketing operations there</u>.

In terms of professional development, we wanted to optimise the training programmes available to our staff because training is vital if we want to remain competitive. <u>As a result, staff</u>

training will no longer be here in Sydney but instead will take place in the Perth office, where new facilities have been installed.

Finally, we've looked at how to optimise our back office administrative functions. Currently, each office has its own admin department. However, this is proving to be less efficient than we would like. In order to resolve this situation, all these functions will now be centralised here in Sydney.

Track 22

Chief Executive Officer:	So what does all this mean for the future? Well, after ten years, I've decided that Benchmark needs a new vision for the future. I think it's time for us to divide up parts of the business into smaller units. Therefore, over the next five years I aim to set up two small subsidiary companies in order to focus on international expansion in Europe and Asia. There are many organisations in emerging markets which could benefit from our experience and skills.
	Which leads me to the next point for future development: that of increasing our workforce. It's become clear that all our departments are understaffed, so we'll be taking on more employees over the next year. And the really good news is that to make us a desirable employer, all positions, current and future, will receive a salary increase of ten per cent.
	Lastly, I know that some people are worried about the financial aspects of having to move to another city as part of the restructure, so Benchmark will be providing a relocation package to all employees thus affected. This is because we would like you all to remain with the company for the foreseeable future.

Tracks 23–27

See page 90 for text.

Track 28

Joe:	Morning, everyone! How are you?
Susan:	Fine thanks, Joe.
Julia:	Yeah, fine, Joe. Have you managed to do much research on our minority languages project?
Joe:	Well, Julia, I've been having some trouble finding information about the number of Cornish speakers in the UK. The records at the Office of National Statistics and the Cornish Language Council say different things, so I'm not sure who to believe.
Julia:	Hm. Susan, have you got any information about this?
Susan:	I was looking on the government's minority languages website, and it says that nearly half the minority language speakers in the UK are speakers of Welsh.
Julia:	Are you sure it's nearly half? I thought the number of Gaelic and Welsh speakers was more or less the same.
Susan:	It used to be, when Gaelic was a compulsory subject in schools. But nowadays there are fewer speakers of Gaelic compared to Welsh. And apparently, with Cornish it's difficult to know the exact percentage of the population who speak it because most people only speak it to intermediate level; very few people are fluent speakers.
Joe:	I suppose that's why the statistics are different. Well, I think we should go with the more conservative estimate based on the number of fluent speakers.
Julia:	I think you're right, which means that Cornish isn't spoken by nearly as many people as the other languages.
Susan:	Yes, I think that's right too. Based on fluent speakers, that means that Welsh is the most widely spoken and the numbers of Irish and Gaelic speakers are more or less the same.

Track 29

Stephanie:	Right, Harry, Rob, shall we get started on this presentation for European Studies?
Rob:	Well, how about if I start by talking about the central regions of Spain, where most people speak Spanish?
Harry:	Good idea. It's important we make it clear that the majority of the population use Spanish as their main language. Then I can introduce the Galician accent of the north-west.
Stephanie:	But isn't Galician more of a dialect?

Harry:	Oh yes, you're right.
Stephanie:	We've got to get our terminology correct because Spain is complicated in terms of languages and dialects and accents. How about we then move across to the north-east, and I give details on the Basque language and how it's different from Spanish.
Rob:	That seems logical, Stephanie. Do you also want to mention the other language in the north-east? It's Catalan, isn't it?
Stephanie:	Yes. In fact we should say it's the official language of the region to show how important it is.
Rob:	So, what am I going to present?
Harry:	We need to include something about accents and speaking styles, don't we?
Rob:	Of course. I could explain the difficulties of understanding the accent in the south due to the fact that the locals speak quickly.
Stephanie:	Excellent! Well I think that covers everything. Shall we meet tomorrow to practise our presentation?

Track 30

Tutor:	So, Natalie, Louise, how are you doing with your report on encouraging people to speak local languages?
Natalie:	Fine thanks, Dr Philips. It's been really interesting.
Louise:	We've found lots of information which we've collated for our report.
Tutor:	Good. What are you going to focus on?
Louise:	Well, many schools and colleges are doing good work promoting local languages both as qualifications and in terms of after-school clubs.
Natalie:	And then there's the rise in popularity of minority language music, which seems to be driven by tourism. Tourists who are exposed to songs in indigenous languages become interested in learning those languages.
Tutor:	OK. Now you need to be careful with these topics. They are fascinating, but you need to look at the influences which drive language learning. Education doesn't leave people much choice, and music isn't a strong enough factor.
Natalie:	Do you have any suggestions for us?
Tutor:	Well, what did we talk about in last week's seminar? Can you remember any of the real push factors?
Louise:	Do you mean things like communication and relationships between companies and their workers?
Tutor:	It's much more powerful than music, don't you think?
Louise:	Yes, I see what you mean. So I suppose our other idea isn't very strong, either. We also thought about hobby groups, but I'm beginning to think they're less significant.
Tutor:	Yes, there aren't sufficient hobbyist groups to make a real difference to local language learning. But, think about something else which is similar but reaches a much larger proportion of the population of a country or community.
Natalie:	Ah! Like online discussion groups? I remember in the lecture you talked about how the Internet is fuelling the increase in local languages through the world languages project.
Tutor:	This is more appropriate for your report because we can actually measure the amount of correspondence in each language and chart increases and decreases over time, which makes it a more rigorous form of analysis.
Natalie:	Of course. So we should definitely include that in our report.
Louise:	It's becoming clearer now. We need to write about the larger factors involving commerce and online communication, where we can record language usage.
Tutor:	I think it's better than looking at anecdotal information.
Louise:	Thanks, Dr Philips.

Track 31

Anna:	So, we need to get this field trip sorted out as soon as possible, don't we?
Suzanne:	Yes. Let's get started. James, have you worked out which two countries we should travel to?
James:	Well, I thought we could go to the USA and Mexico because that's where the populations of most native languages are concentrated. But then I found out that the three languages we're most interested in are more widely spoken in Canada than Mexico so I think we should go there instead.
Suzanne:	OK ... Anna, weren't you going to think about our research focus?
Anna:	Yes, and I think I've found two areas that would work well. Firstly, use of the three languages, Na-Dene, Salishan, and Algic among the younger generation – people up to the age of twenty-five.

	I found out that although there are many older speakers of Algic, it's used much less by the young. In fact young people under the age of twenty-five use both Na-Dene and Salishan more than Algic.
James:	That's interesting. That means that native language use isn't really being affected by the older generations any more.
Suzanne:	So, what's the other focus area then, Anna?
Anna:	Well, it would be good to try to find out what affects changes in native language speaker populations.
James:	You mean things like family life, and the influence of popular culture or tourism?
Anna:	Yes, areas like that, but not tourism or culture because they're too general. I think we should look at whether family has an impact in terms of passing on native language use. And possibly the effects of government language policy too.
Suzanne:	Government figures can be deceptive, but they're still worth looking at. Maybe we should also focus on something like job creation and work statistics and the number of people who leave the USA to live in another country instead.
James:	Mm, yes. I think emigration would be as useful as language policy.
Suzanne:	OK, then. Let's focus on those three as well as what happens in families.

Track 32

Anna:	Well, shall we look at our route now? Most of the speakers we're looking for are in California, so we could start there. We can spend two weeks travelling around and meeting people to get some background information and then start collecting data.
Suzanne:	What do you think about beginning in the south-west corner of the state and visiting the Barona reservation?
Anna:	That's a good idea. We'll be able to get some interviews with native language speakers there. And then we could go to the eastern mountains to visit the local education authority of North County – they've got a native language project for school children.
James:	Why there? Wouldn't it be better to go to the education department in San Diego? It's bigger.
Anna:	But they focus more on Spanish and English bilingualism and less on native languages.
James:	In that case, the North County Education Authority will be more valuable so let's do that. After that, we could head south-east to the town of Bishop. There's a company there called Co-Tech, which employs only bilingual speakers. I've emailed the managing director, who's happy to give us an interview.
Suzanne:	That's great work, James! It sounds like something we should definitely do.
James:	Right, well I'll email her to confirm.
Anna:	Also, we should go to Sun City. It's this bilingual town in the south central area of the region. They have a policy whereby all signs in the town must be in the local language as well as English. We can take photos of these signs – they'll make good visuals for our report.
Suzanne:	But won't that be intrusive for the people who live there?
Anna:	No, they're used to it – the village is used as a model for other communities who'd like to do the same thing.
Suzanne:	In that case, let's add it to the itinerary.

Track 33

Ellen:	Excuse me, where are the dresses?
Assistant:	They're at the end of this aisle, on the left. Can I help you with anything?
Ellen:	Yes, maybe. I'm not from around here, so I don't know this store.
Assistant:	Well, I can help you with anything you need.
Ellen:	Fantastic. I'm actually down here for my brother's wedding, and I need something to wear. I've just started a new job and I haven't had time to get anything yet. I'm looking for something smart. Maybe a new dress.
Assistant:	Well what about this one?
Ellen:	I think it's too hot for long sleeves.
Assistant:	Yes, well, this one has shorter sleeves, and it still has the bow, which I think is a nice detail. Or there's this patterned one?

Ellen:	I'm not keen on a pattern. I think I'll go for the one with the bow. Do you have it in a size 10?
Assistant:	Let me have a look ... Yes, here.
Ellen:	Great! I need a hat, and then I can try them on together.
Assistant:	What kind of hat are you looking for?
Ellen:	What about this one with the flower?
Assistant:	Yes, but if I may suggest, a taller hat would add to your height.
Ellen:	Really?
Assistant:	Yes, try this one.
Ellen:	I see what you mean!
Assistant:	We have this style with the single flower, or with a small bunch. And it comes with a wide or narrow brim.
Ellen:	I like the narrow brim, and just the one flower. Hmm, can I have a blue flower?
Assistant:	I'm afraid it just comes in cream.
Ellen:	Well ... it goes with the dress, anyway.
Assistant:	Great. I'll place an order and have the hat sent to you. It'll take about two days to be delivered. Is that OK?
Ellen:	Yes, that's fine.
Assistant:	I need to take down a few details for delivery. Can I take your name?
Ellen:	Ellen Barker.
Assistant:	And the delivery address?
Ellen:	It'll be my brother's address. It's 15 ... no ... 14 Brightwell Avenue.
Assistant:	14 ... Can you spell that, please?
Ellen:	Yes. B–R–I–G–H–T–W–E–L–L Avenue, Staybridge, Kent, DA4 7DF
Assistant:	And can I take a contact number?
Ellen:	Yes, my mobile is 03221 7774 (0–3–double 2–1–triple 7–4).
Assistant:	03221 7775.
Ellen:	No, it's a 4 at the end.
Assistant:	Sorry. I've got it now. We can deliver on May the twelfth. We can't specify an exact time, just morning or afternoon.
Ellen:	Any time in the early morning is fine.
Assistant:	And how would you like to pay?
Ellen:	Visa
Assistant:	Great. That comes to £32.25.
Ellen:	Okay, thanks.

Track 34

Ellen:	I'm just going to try this dress on and then look for shoes. Where are the changing rooms?
Assistant:	They're to the left of the store, right next to Customer Services.
Ellen:	And I want some shoes and accessories, too. Where can I find them?
Assistant:	The accessories are in the Womenswear department. The shoe department is right at the front of the store, between Menswear and Home Furnishings. Oh, no, sorry ... We've just moved the shoe department for the summer season. It's now very near the changing rooms, actually, straight in front of them.
Ellen:	Thanks so much for your help. And where can I pay for the other things?
Assistant:	The cash desk is at the front of the store, by the Menswear.
Ellen:	Thanks.

Track 35

Tour guide:	Welcome to San Fernando City Tours. I'm Mark, your tour guide. We have a lot to see in three hours, so make sure you're comfortable! We'll be travelling into the historical district first, and then into the town centre. After that, it's out to the harbour, and we'll finish up at the lighthouse, just past the harbour. That will take us up to midday, and after that, you're free to do what you want. At the lighthouse you'll have a chance to visit the tea room and take photographs of the magnificent coastline. Now, as we have only three hours, we won't be able to take you round

the shopping district, but we think you'd prefer to look around the shops there in your own time, anyway.

San Fernando has some well-known tourist attractions – the lighthouse for example, and the National Library. However, the little-known Military Museum is not to be missed. Be sure to visit before you leave!

Now, there's a lot to do in San Fernando. Indeed, there really *is* something for everyone! For those who love the water, I can recommend a trip on the Seafarer, one of the most famous boats on the San Fernando River. It does an evening trip with a three-course meal included. It's great fun for everyone, but especially for young people in their teens or twenties – after nine there's a disco on the boat and it gets really lively! Then there's a climbing wall near the town centre. It's incredibly popular, with a large wall for expert climbers, and a smaller wall for novices. There's also a junior wall and a crèche, so it's a great day out for those of you with kids. And if you like walking, there are some great walking tours. The City Sights Tour is highly recommended, as is the walking tour by the coast. But that one's only for the fit, not really suitable for children or the elderly. For more mature people or those less able to get around, I would suggest a tour around the vineyards. It can be done in the luxury of a coach, and it's a wonderful way to explore the region's wines.

Track 36

Tour guide: Naturally, there's a charge for all these attractions, but you can get fifteen per cent off if you have an Explorer Pass. If you don't have a pass but would like one, the driver here has application forms. Just ask him for one and fill it out while on the tour. Then you hand it in to the tour office. Normally, it costs $10, but this year it's just $7! When you hand it in, you'll get your picture taken for the card on the spot, and then your card is ready to use! Remember to show it whenever you pay for anything! The discounts apply not just to tourist attractions, but some bars and restaurants. Basically, everywhere you see a red explorer symbol.

Ah ... We're coming up to the historical district now ...

Track 37

Tutor:	Hi, Katie. Hi, Ian. Come on in!
Katie:	Hi, Professor Gordon. We wanted to talk to you about our wildlife presentation next week.
Tutor:	Have you decided how to organise it?
Ian:	Yes, Professor. At first, we were going to focus on the cat family, but then we decided to talk about nocturnal animals instead.
Tutor:	Yes, good idea. And how is your planning going?
Katie:	It's going well. We think we have enough material for twenty minutes. The advantage is that there are so many visual aids we can use. We've found lots on the Internet which we think will be really interesting for people.
Ian:	The problem is that this topic has been hard to narrow down. If anything, we've got too much information for just twenty minutes. How do you think we could narrow it down further?
Tutor:	It is a broad subject. There are a few ways you could do it, but I'd recommend just looking at a representative sample of nocturnal animals, just four or five.
Ian:	Yes, and maybe we could choose one animal from each continent, or a land creature, a marine creature and a winged animal.
Katie:	I like the idea of separating it by different types of animals. And if we limit the detail, we'll definitely have enough time!
Tutor:	But don't limit the detail too much. Also, think how you're going to interest the audience.
Katie:	Well, we're going to have a picture for each animal so we can talk through the picture.
Tutor:	That's a nice idea, but don't limit yourself to pictures. If you can find any clips of the animals, use them! Showing brief video clips can keep an audience interested.
Ian:	I'll look on the Internet tonight.
Tutor:	And think of questions to ask your audience. People like to be involved!
Katie:	Yes, that's a great idea. Anyway, Professor, we've been practising our presentation and we'd like to show you a small section. Is that OK?
Tutor:	Well, we just have a couple of minutes left, but go ahead!

Track 38

Katie: Well, we were thinking of presenting each animal with a picture and describing their physical characteristics.

Tutor: OK, but not in too much detail. That's just background information.

Ian: We'll start with the jaguar. I'll introduce it by saying that the jaguar is a nocturnal animal and the only species of the genus *Panthera* to be found in the Americas. Like any cat, it has whiskers and it can move quickly. Its spine has great movement, meaning a jaguar can take long strides, sometimes up to five and a half metres. This can make it a deadly predator as you can imagine! Moving on to the fur ... Its fur is quite distinct. The markings are like black doughnut-shaped spots on its otherwise yellow fur. People often confuse them with the leopard for this reason. Now the tail is interesting. Although people think that the tail has stripes on it, the fur on the tail actually is similar to the body with black circles around the lower section. The jaguar is generally a creature to be feared. ... Oh, yes, I should have mentioned this earlier. Sorry. Like most cats, it has sharp, retractable claws.

Tutor: Yes, that's fine, but be careful. The jaguar is usually thought of as nocturnal, but strictly speaking, it's crepuscular, in other words, most active between dusk and dawn. But as long as you mention this, you can put it under the umbrella of nocturnal. Is that all?

Katie: Yes, I think so. Thanks, Professor.

Track 39

Lecturer: The subject of this series of lectures is horology, the science of measuring time, and we'll be looking at a few basic concepts in this lecture.

The measurement of time has come a long way since ancient times. It began with such devices as the sundial, where the position of the sun's shadow marked the hour. Daylight was divided into twelve 'temporary hours' – these temporary hours were longer in the summer and shorter in the winter, simply because the amount of daylight changes with the seasons.

The earliest sundial we know comes from Egypt. It was made of stone and is thought to date from 1500 BC. Sundials were used throughout the classical world, and with time, evolved into more elaborate devices that could take into account seasonal changes and geographical positioning and reflect the hours accurately, no matter what the time of year. This was quite an achievement in technology. Today, sundials can be seen as decorative pieces in many gardens.

In the eleventh century, the Chinese invented the first mechanical clocks. They were large and expensive, and certainly not intended for individuals. However, this is the type of clock we are familiar with today. There have been many developments in clocks and watches since then, and they have been greatly improved, but if your clock or watch makes a ticking sound, then it could well be based on the mechanical movements the Chinese developed a thousand years ago!

However, timekeeping has moved on from the mechanical clock. Time has become so important that there is a series of atomic clocks around the world which measure International Atomic Time. Even though many countries have their own calendars, globalisation has made it essential that we measure time uniformly, so that we know, for example, that when it's 6 a.m. in the United Kingdom, it's 2 p.m. in Beijing. This standard was set in 1958. Now these atomic clocks are situated in over seventy laboratories all over the world.

There is so much to cover about the development of time measurement that I would like to refer you to the reading list. The core text is *The Development of Time: Theory and Practice*, but there are many other useful texts. A good grounding in the subject is given in *Understanding Time* by J. R. Beale. Although some sections lack detailed analyses, it does offer a good foundation. Also *Time: Concepts and Conventions* is quite a useful read. You might think from the title that it is about the philosophy of time, but this isn't the case. Rather, it gives a good description of how different countries have different approaches to time in terms of calendars and days. Lastly, *The Story of Time* by David Harris analyses time in great detail, and I would recommend this book if you are aiming to specialise in horology.

Now, we're going to continue with an in-depth look at lunar and solar cycles.

Answer key

1   On the move

Part 1:   Vocabulary

Exercise 1
a 6,   b 7,   c 8,   d 2,   e 3,   f 1,   g 5,   h 4

Exercise 2
1 h,   2 c/g,   3 f,   4 a,   5 b/f,   6 d,   7 c/g,   8 e/f

Exercise 3
1 f,   2 a,   3 d,   4 h,   5 c,   6 g,   7 e,   8 b

Exercise 4
1 c,   2 c,   3 a,   4 b

Part 2:   Practice exercises

Exercise 1

Predictions
1 name of place (e.g. country, city),   2 time (e.g. 2 weeks/1 month/weekend),   3 description/ types of holiday (e.g. beach/city break/relaxing/ sightseeing),   4 Mexico,   5 6 weeks   6 working

Exercise 2

Predictions
1 time period (e.g. 2 weeks/1 month),   2 person (e.g. friend/family member/school mate),   3 verb (e.g. *speak/learn*),   4 2 weeks,   5 best friend,   6 to study

Exercise 3
1 name,   2 place,   3 time,   4 date

Exercise 4
1 name,   2 time,   3 name,   4 date,
5 time,   6 name,   7 date

Exercise 5
1 GEOFFREY,   2 19th September,   3 210,   4 cash

Exercise 6
1 c,   2 d,   3 a,   4 a,   5 b,   6 d

Exercise 7
1 a,   2 c,   3 d,   4 b

Exercise 8
(Suggested answers)
a John is poorly. / John is sick.
b He has arranged to see a play. / He has got tickets for a musical.
c He is afraid of being on the water. / He is frightened of the sea.

Exercise 9
1 c (Look at the audioscript on page 103. John has *booked theatre tickets*, but this is not the reason he cannot go on the boat trip. The reason is that he is scared of water: *I hate the sea, and I'll be sick with fear if the waves are big!* The word *sick* is used here, but John is saying he will be sick because he is scared, not because he is ill.)

Exercise 10
1 c,   2 c

Part 3:   Exam practice

Questions 1–4
1 Carter,   2 636197,   3 Riverside Hotel,   4 2.00/2/two

Questions 5–6
5 A,   6 C

Questions 7–10
7 D,   8 A,   9 C,   10 B

2   Being young

Part 1:   Vocabulary

Exercise 1
a 1, 2,   b 1,   c 1,   d 3,   e 2

Exercise 2
1 a,   2 c,   3 b,   4 e,   5 d

Exercise 3
1 motivation,   2 motivated/motivating/motivational,   3 practise,   4 practice,   5 succeed,   6 success,   7 successful,   8 instruct,   9 instructive/instructional,   10 instructively/instructionally,   11 concentration,   12 concentrated,   13 capability,   14 capably,   15 express,   16 expression,   17 expressively

Exercise 4
1 active,   2 act,   3 activities,   4 actively

Exercise 5
1 active,   2 concentrate,   3 instructor,   4 practise,   5 practice,   6 motivates,   7 concentration,   8 active,   9 successful

Part 2:   Practice exercises

Exercise 1
1 b (The names of languages are capitalised, so 'French' is correct.)
2 e (The full name is given for the previous student in the table.)
3 h (The percentage symbol (%) is already included so you cannot include it again. If you write the percentage in words, it is more than two words and does not follow the format.)

Exercise 2

1 Angela,   2 10.50 ('Ten pounds fifty' is incorrect because the instructions say 'write no more than two words'.),   3 Tango,   4 Wednesday,   5 10.00

Exercise 3

1 5–10,   2 online dangers,   3 friends (online),
4 Test Doctors

Exercise 4

a 2,   b 1,   c 1,   d 2,   e 3,   f 3

Exercise 5

1 cabins,   2 tents,   3 cooking area

Exercise 6

1 Chart B,   2 Chart A

Exercise 7

Chart A

1 Get a team of 7 players,   2 Elect a captain,
3 Fill in an application,   4 Pay entrance
fee,   5 Dates and times sent,   6 Confirm
attendance,   7 Receive opening event invitation

Chart B

1 Complete admission form
1b If not a member, join the club
2 Pay deposit
3 Receive confirmation later

Exercise 8

1 youth club,   2 welcome pack,   3 Coordinator/
Co-ordinator,   4 record book,   5 badge

Part 3:   Exam Practice

Questions 1–4
1 Salsa,   2 Jim,   3 Football,
4 Roller skating/Roller-skating

Questions 5–7
5 Dance Studios,   6 Changing Rooms,   7 Tennis Courts

Questions 8–10
8 sign,   9 reception,   10 membership card

3   Climate

Part 1:   Vocabulary

Exercise 1
a 4,   b 2,   c 5,   d 6,   e 1,   f 3

Exercise 2
1 glaciers,   2 salinity,   3 humidity,
4 kilometres (*British English*)/kilometers
(*American English*),   5 pressure,   6 evaporation,
7 environment,   8 biology,   9 brightness

Exercise 3
1 c/e,   2 g,   3 b,   4 c,   5 a,   6 h,   7 d,   8 f

Exercise 4

1 'Atmosphere' is different: the other
   words relate to water.

2 'Ozone layer' is different: it denotes
   a layer of the atmosphere while the
   other words describe a change.

3 'Tidal wave' is different: it relates to the sea
   while the other words denote kinds of wind.

4 'Drizzle' is different: it denotes light rain
   while the other words relate to water in
   the atmosphere that affect visibility.

Exercise 5
Before: former, initially, previously, prior
After: eventually, finally, in the end, next,
the next phase/step, ultimately, when
At the same time: during, simultaneously, when
Transition from one stage to another: moving
on to, next, the next phase/step, when
Notes:

- If two clauses agree in tense, *when* shows
  that an event occurs simultaneously with another
  one. For example: *When the wind blows, it is
  cold.* (when + present + present) With words like
  finish and *stop*, this indicates a time change.

- If the two clauses do not agree, then there is
  a time change. For example: *When it has been
  hot all summer, the harvest is usually abundant.*
  (when + present perfect + present simple)

- Note the two uses of *next*. Sometimes
  there is a clear indication of transition,
  sometimes there is not. For example:
  *The clouds got dark and next it was
  raining heavily.* (transition)
  I'll meet you next week. (i.e. *I'll meet you after this
  week.* – There is no context to give it transition.)

Exercise 6
1 d,   2 e,   3 a,   4 h,   5 b,   6 c,   7 f,   8 g

Exercise 7
1 eventually,   2 prior,   3 when,   4 Initially,
5 Next,   6 ultimately, eventually

Part 2:   Practice exercises

Exercise 1
Steven 1,   Joanne 2

Exercise 2
1 c,   2 a,   3 b,   4 a,   5 b,   6 c

Exercise 3
1 a,   2 b,   3 c,   4 a,   5 c

Exercise 4
c, a, b, d

Exercise 5
1 power plants,   2 natural events,
3 (acidic) compounds,   4 snow or fog

Exercise 6

1 verb, 2 noun, 3 verb, 4 noun, 5 quantity/amount

Exercise 7

1 rains, 2 (any) electrical equipment,
3 crouch down, 4 first aider, 5 80%/eighty per cent

Part 3: Exam practice

Questions 1–3

1 research/our own research/own research,
2 wide reaching/wide-reaching, 3 break down

Questions 4–7

4 D, 5 C, 6 B, 7 A

Questions 8–10

8 rotate/spin, 9 lose, 10 (around) the other direction

4 Family structures

Part 1: Vocabulary

Exercise 1

a 2, b 3, c 1, d 4

Exercise 2

1 relation/relative, 2 marry, 3 parent, 4 inheritance,
5 household, 6 engaged, 7 adopt, 8 cousin

Exercise 3

1 e/i, 2 b, 3 d, 4 h, 5 i/e, 6 j, 7 g,
8 c, 9 a, 10 f

Exercise 4

1 agree with, 2 cares for, 3 disapprove of,
4 aimed at (passive construction), 5 struggle with,
6 participate in, 7 refer to, 8 concentrates on

Exercise 5

1 parent, 2 concentrating, 3 engaged, 4 step,
5 extended, 6 household, 7 cousins, 8 for, 9 suffer

Part 2: Practice exercises

Exercise 1

1 e, 2 f, 3 a, 4 g, 5 b, 6 h, 7 d, 8 c

Exercise 2

Order: firstly, lastly, next
Reason: the reason for this is, due to
Result: as a result, thus
Repetition: in other words
Contrast: however, on the other hand
Addition: also, furthermore, in addition
Example: a case in point is, an illustration of
this is, for example, for instance
Emphasis: the main point is, the crucial factor
is, what I am essentially arguing is

Exercise 3

1 b, 2 f, 3 h, 4 a, 5 d, 6 e, 7 g, 8 c

Exercise 4

1 On average, when do people get married?
2 What is the key reason given for the
increase in divorce numbers?
3 Who believe that families are the key to
the functioning of wider society?
4 What is the average number of
family members in the UK?
1 a, e, 2 d, h, i, 3 c, f 4 b, g, j

Exercise 5

1 What percentage of women in their early
thirties still live with their parents?
2 When were house prices only three
times the average yearly income?
3 What is the reason that people return to
their parental home after university?
4 Who does the Affordable Housing
Scheme aim to help?
1 5%/5 per cent/five per cent
2 1980s/nineteen eighties (Note: '1980' would
not be a correct answer. The speaker
is referring to the entire decade.)
3 student debt
4 first time buyers/first-time buyers

Exercise 6
Suggested answers:

1 adjective, 2 'to' + noun/noun phrase (to express
reason), 3 present simple/past simple verb ('often' is
usually used with the present or past simple),
4 words used to indicate percentage/amount + 'of'
1 traditional, 2 to property ownership,
3 inherit, 4 a third of

Exercise 7

1 Families lived with servants.
2 Children were mainly home schooled.
3 Fathers occasionally taught their children Latin.
4 The Victorians were not generous to the poor.
5 Parents were strict with their children.

Exercise 8

1 c, 2 a, 3 e, 4 b, 5 f, d

Exercise 9

d, e

Part 3: Exam practice

Questions 1–4

1 nuclear family, 2 a step family,
3 to separate, 4 consumer spending

Questions 5–8

5 1 in 4/ one in four, 6 Women, 7 married,
8 (in) rented accommodation

Questions 9–10

9 B/D, 10 B/D

5   Starting university

Part 1:   Vocabulary

Exercise 1
1 student: The other words are people who teach.
2 presentation: The other words are written forms of assessment; a presentation is spoken.
3 brochure: This is the only non-academic printed material.
4 lesson: The other words are university styles of teaching; a lesson takes place in a school.

Exercise 2
1 tutorials,   2 student,   3 lecturers,   4 presentations

Exercise 3
1 astronomy,   2 philosophically,   3 sociological,
4 statistician,   5 politics,   6 biologist,   7 economic (= concerned with the organization of the money, industry, and trade of a country, region, or society)/economical (= not requiring a lot of money to operate),   8 physicist

Exercise 4
1 politicians,   2 philosophical,   3 statistics,
4 physics,   5 astronomer

Exercise 5
1 N,   2 A,   3 AD,   4 NP,   5 A,   6 N,   7 NP,   8 A

Exercise 6
1 enjoyable,   2 supervisor,   3 helpful,
4 effectively,   5 manageable,   6 scientific

Part 2:   Practice exercises

Exercise 1
Suggested answers:
1 easy, fun, interesting, fascinating, challenging
2 good, very good, excellent, knowledgeable, competent
3 alone, on her own, by herself, without other people
4 fail, not pass, do badly in, struggle with

Exercise 2
1 not that difficult,   2 (highly) knowledgeable,
3 alone,   4 not pass

Exercise 3
1 d,   2 a,   3 e,   4 c,   5 b

Exercise 4
a 4,   b 2,   c 3,   d 1,   e 5

Exercise 5
1 bowling alley,   2 park,   3 (Elm Tree/Elmtree) Café,   4 swimming baths,   5 leisure centre

Exercise 6
1 78A High Trees Street, Sydney, 2316
2 354 Castle Avenue, Edinburgh, E5 7HU
3 86 The Drive, Brooklyn, New York, 45008

Exercise 7
1 Taylor,   2 Mathematics,   3 Ashley,   4 M4 9JA

Exercise 8
1 8/eight books,   2 molecular biology,
3 in person,   4 (personal) tutor

Exercise 9
1 social,   2 accommodation,   3 (on) student card

Part 3:   Exam practice

Questions 1–4
1 AND105763,   2 Earth Science,   3 Lavender,   4 566341

Questions 5–7
5 Training,   6 Philosophy,   7 TV room

Questions 8–10
8 online reservation system,
9 (student) number,   10 email

6   Fame

Part 1:   Vocabulary

Exercise 1
1 c,   2 a,   3 f,   4 d,   5 b,   6 e

Exercise 2
1 programmes/shows,   2 scripts,   3 flexible,
4 creative,   5 star,   6 acting,   7 press/media,   8 play,
9 character,   10 international,   11 shot/filmed,
12 location,   13 unimaginable,   14 post-production

Exercise 3
1 counter-productive,   2 semi-final,
3 multinational,   4 recreate,   5 bilingual

Exercise 4
1 inequality,   2 distrust,   3 imperfect,
4 irresponsible,   5 unaware

Exercise 5
1 ir(regular),   2 multi-(million),   3 un(likely),
4 re-(think),   5 ir(responsible),   6 un(reasonable)

Part 2:   Practice exercises

Exercise 1
1 composed,   2 nationally,   3 performance,
4 creatively,   5 last,   6 first night/opening/opening night,   7 award,   8 sacked/dismissed

Exercise 2
1 vii,   2 i/vi,   3 i/vi,   4 ii/iv,   5 ii/iv,   6 v

Exercise 3
1 d (She died in 1968 and you can see her gravestone in Tanbridge Cemetery.)

2 b (A bestselling horror writer, he got many of his themes for his haunting novels from this very town.)

3 a (Not only a poet, he has also written ten novels that have topped the book sales charts.)

4 c (Before she headed for Hollywood, you could have seen her waiting tables in The Dorage Restaurant here in town!)

Exercise 4

Answer: c (The book 'tells the story'. He read the story, and made the film from that story.

Incorrect answers:

a: South America was where he was inspired, but the film was not based on his travels.

b: Chambers heard about a book or novel. He was not told the story.

Exercise 5

1 b (He claims his inspiration for the film is his own experiences growing up in 1950s Liverpool.)

Incorrect answers:

a (The text mentions stories, but only to say that the director 'still thinks the majority of ghost stories are actually true'.)

c (The film 'has the feel of a comic book', but it is not based on one.)

2 b ('What Happens in the Night' is a film that will scare you. I wouldn't say it's the best horror film to come out this year, but it's certainly shot beautifully, and it's not hard to follow.)

Incorrect answers:

a ('What Happens in the Night' is a film that will scare you. I wouldn't say it's the best horror film to come out this year, but it's certainly shot beautifully, and it's not hard to follow.)

c ('What Happens in the Night' is a film that will scare you. I wouldn't say it's the best horror film to come out this year, but it's certainly shot beautifully, and it's not hard to follow.)

3 a (Rumour has it that Smith and Wyatt aren't the best of friends. In fact, on the set they barely spoke to each other!)

Incorrect answers:

b (The stars are in love in the film, but not in real life.)

c (Rumour has it that Smith and Wyatt aren't the best of friends. In fact, on the set they barely spoke to each other!)

4 b (If you want romance, this film is fine)

Incorrect answers:

a (The reviewer says that 'men and women alike can get something from this film', but she doesn't actually recommend it for women, as opposed to me,)

c (The reviewer implies that Happy as Larry is not a particularly good film: 'Happy as

Larry is a move away from the usual films Sonya makes – she is better known for her roles in action films – but she has shown herself to be a capable comedy actress. However, I'm not sure this is the finest film to do it in.')

Exercise 6

Correct:

a (Sentence iv: 'the number ... has almost doubled' corresponds to 'More people'; 'celebrities' corresponds to 'famous [people]')

c (Sentence v: 'All aspects of a celebrity's life' corresponds to 'almost everything about famous people'; 'are made known to the public' corresponds to 'The public now know')

e (Sentence ii: 'People are now famous' corresponds to 'Fame'; 'for only short periods' corresponds to 'more short-lived')

Exercise 7

Answers can be given in any order.

1–3:

a (It's true that there are more celebrities around than ever before.)

c (Famous people are everywhere and although we know nearly all there is to know about these people – their lives are splashed all over magazines and television – they've retained their mystery.)

d (One day a person is famous and the next they are forgotten.)

4–6:

b (In fact, the paparazzi, who photograph the rich and famous, are often seen as figures of hate for this. They come off much worse in the end, because they are so disliked by the public and celebrities.)

d (And who pays for this? Well, all of us. Cinema and concert ticket prices have risen and DVDs cost more than ever.)

e (... the rewards go to only a small elite ... but they miss a lot of the creative talent in the industry, like the people who write the screenplays. They are still on the same salary they were on ten years ago.)

Part 3: Exam practice

Questions 1–3

Answers can be given in any order.

B, F (The scheme has been great for tourism, but it was really started to raise awareness of the rich history of Sydney, [B] both locally [F] and nationally, and we think we've managed to do this.)

C (We also wanted to make people aware of the impressive list of important people who have lived in this city, and we've certainly achieved that.)

Incorrect answers:

A (Tourism has benefited, but this was not one of the reasons for starting the scheme: 'The scheme has been great for tourism, but it was really started to raise awareness of the rich history of Sydney ...)

D (The scheme has been good for publicity, but publicity was not one of the original aims.)

E (Again, the scheme has helped to preserve old buildings but it was not one of the reasons for starting the scheme: 'Although not part of our original aims, the scheme has also helped preserve some of the older and more important buildings in Sydney'.)

Questions 4–6

4 C (It has been really wonderful in highlighting our past.)

Incorrect answers:

A (Although the scheme has helped tourism, we do not know if has actually increased the amount of tourism in the area.)

B (There is no mention of people who have become better known as a result of the scheme.)

5 C (A plaque can only be given to a person who is famous and has achieved something out of the ordinary, like an important politician or world-record-breaking sportsman for example.)

A (If you want to nominate someone for a plaque you just need the person's name, where they lived and you need three signatures to approve your application.)

B (The role of the panel is to check that the data submitted is correct, not to approve nominations: 'Our panel then checks that all the data you've submitted is correct and hopefully, within a year a new plaque will be erected.')

6 A (Whereas in the past the tourist board put in the majority of funding, now public donations count for sixty-five per cent of all total funds!)

Questions 7–10

7 D (For example, if they are interested in famous sports personalities they can do a tour following the red plaques (the colour we are aiming to use for these people).)

8 A (We are thinking of using grey plaques to signify people who have done important work within the government ...)

9 B (We are thinking of using ... white plaques for those who have done good works in the community.)

10 E (Lastly, our green plaques we think will be very popular, these will be for painters and sculptors)

7 Alternative energy

Part 1: Vocabulary

Exercise 1
Nouns: chemical, electricity, fuel, gas, heat, liquid, metal, oil, oxygen, substance
Verbs: boil, burn, cool, freeze, fuel, gas, heat, melt, oil
Adjectives: chemical, cool, nuclear, solar

Exercise 2
1 An effective way of producing power is to use solar energy.
2 At the North and South Poles, water becomes so cold that it freezes.
3 If you heat water to 100 degrees Centigrade, it boils.
4 This power station uses nuclear energy to generate electricity.
5 Oil is a substance found under the surface of the earth.
6 In order to make a fire, some kind of fuel such as wood is needed.
7 If you oil an engine, it will function more effectively.
8 Refrigeration is the main method of cooling food.

Exercise 3
1 e, 2 c, 3 f, 4 b, 5 i, 6 a, 7 h, 8 d, 9 j, 10 g

Exercise 4
1 confirmed/announced/claimed, 2 denied,
3 recommended, 4 warned, 5 persuaded

Exercise 5
1 b, 2 d, 3 h, 4 i, 5 g, 6 a, 7 e, 8 f, 9 c

Part 2: Practice exercises

Exercise 1
1 A, 2 A, 3 U, 4 D, 5 D,
6 A, 7 U, 8 D/U, 9 A, 10 U

Exercise 2
Dialogue 1: Yes.
A: I think we should visit the nuclear power station as part of our research for this module.
B: I couldn't agree more. And hopefully, we'll be able to interview some of the staff for a more in-depth view of how it works.

Dialogue 2: Yes.
A: Geothermal energy is the best option for governments to invest in for the future.
B: Mm, I'm with you on that, but like all things it depends on the amount of investment.

Dialogue 3: No, the second speaker is not sure.
A: <u>What I particularly like</u> about using hydrogen as energy is that it is environmentally friendly.
B: Well, I haven't seen any reports to support that so <u>I wouldn't like to say</u>.

Exercise 3
1 S,   2 M,   3 M,   4 S,   5 M,   6 S

Exercise 4
1 general,   2 specific,   3 make notes,
4 (kind of) system,   5 relevance

Exercise 5
1 The answers will be verbs or nouns which refer to methods.
   Possible answers: use/using less lighting, turn/turning down heating, recycle/recycling
2 The answers will be types of fuels which can be seen as negative.
   Possible answers: carbon dioxide, oil, gas, nuclear waste
3 solar (energy), biofuels, nuclear (energy)

Exercise 6
1 background details,   2 diagrams

Exercise 7
1 j, k, l (The word must be a noun that refers to a type of academic discussion.)
2 a, c, e, g (The word must be an adjective because it comes before the noun 'energy'. Note that in terms of context, only a, c and g are possible.)
3 a, c, e (The word must be an adjective because it comes before the noun phrase 'energy source'.)
4 b, d, f, h, i, (The word must be a noun because there is an article 'the' before it. Note that in terms of the context, only d and i are possible.)
5 f, j (The word must be a singular or uncountable noun because there is an adjective before it ('academic') and the verb 'appears' is singular.)

Exercise 8
1 l,   2 c,   3 h,   4 a,   5 f

Part 3:   Exam practice

Questions 1–4
1 less reliable,   2 (generally/very) expensive (to produce),   3 critical analysis,   4 wide reading

Questions 5–7
5 daylight,   6 country,   7 willing to

Questions 8–10
8 G,   9 C,   10 B

8   Migration

Part 1:   Vocabulary

Exercise 1
1 i,   2 j,   3 f,   4 c,   5 h,   6 g,   7 a,
8 l,   9 k,   10 b,   11 d,   12 e

Exercise 2
1 migrating,   2 monarch,   3 colony,
4 heritage,   5 Overpopulation,   6 Demographic

Exercise 3
Change in appearance: restore, distorted, manipulated, shrank
Change in quality: restore, amended, manipulated, deteriorated, distorted
Change in quantity: manipulated, boomed, diminished, eradicated, shrank, tailed off

Part 2:   Practice exercises

Exercise 1
1 ci-<u>vi</u>-lian,   2 de-mo-<u>gra</u>-phic,   3 in-<u>di</u>-ge-nous,
4 mi-<u>gra</u>-tion,   5 po-pu-<u>la</u>-tion,   6 <u>he</u>-ri-tage,
7 <u>an</u>-ces-tor,   8 chro-no-<u>lo</u>-gi-cally,   9 <u>co</u>-lo-ny,
10 co-<u>lo</u>-ni-al-is-m

Exercise 2
The words which are stressed most often in English are verbs, nouns, adverbs and adjectives because these are the content words which contain most of the meaning of a sentence.
1 Due to the <u>increasing number</u> of <u>people</u> <u>moving abroad</u> for <u>work purposes</u>, <u>home</u> is something that is <u>difficult</u> to <u>define</u>.
2 One of the <u>most important factors</u> which <u>causes people</u> to <u>move</u> to a <u>different city</u> or <u>country</u> is <u>employment</u>.
3 <u>Migration</u> has been <u>occurring</u> since the <u>beginning</u> of <u>humankind's habitation</u> of the <u>planet</u> and is likely to <u>continue</u> for many <u>generations</u> to <u>come</u>.
4 The <u>indigenous people</u> of <u>South America</u> have not <u>changed</u> their <u>way</u> of <u>life</u> for <u>centuries</u> and <u>continue</u> to <u>resist</u> the <u>effects</u> of <u>globalisation</u>.
5 Our <u>ancestors</u> were <u>nomadic people</u> who <u>moved</u> from <u>place</u> to <u>place</u> in search of <u>food</u> and shelter.

Exercise 3
The list of families is more likely to be paraphrased because the list a–c contains names of places, which cannot be changed. In classification questions, names of people or places or specific objects will usually not be paraphrased.

Suggested answers:
1 Families with average incomes / Families who are comfortable financially
2 Wealthy couples without children / Rich childless families
3 Couples who no longer work / People who receive a pension / Those in retirement
4 Families with low incomes / Families who work in blue collar jobs
5 Wealthy households / Families who are very well off

Exercise 4
1 c,   2 c,   3 a,   4 a,   5 b

Exercise 5
1 e,   2 b,   3 a,   4 d,   5 f,   6 c

Exercise 6
1 being suspicious/suspicious of people,
2 beliefs and values,   3 listen,   4 isolation

Exercise 7
The <u>1844 Naturalisation Act</u> was designed to <u>know more about immigrants</u> as they had to <u>give their personal information when they arrived</u> in Britain.
(Suggested answers)
When immigrants arrived in Britain, they had to give their personal information under the 1844 Naturalisation Act so that the government could find out more about them. /
   So that the government could find out more about them, when immigrants arrived in Britain, they had to give their personal information under the 1844 Naturalisation Act.

Exercise 8
1 register,   2 5/five years,   3 spies,
4 British Nationality,   5 work permits

Part 3: Exam practice

Questions 1–3
1 sent home,   2 Legal examination,   3 Ferry

Questions 4–6
4 a,   5 d,   6 c

Questions 7–10
7 shipbuilding,   8 2.3 million,
9 Brooklyn Bridge,   10 restoration

9   At the gym

Part 1:   Vocabulary

Exercise 1
1 instructor,   2 recommendations,   3 running,
4 healthy,   5 exercising,   6 fit

Exercise 2
1 d,   2 f,   3 b,   4 h,   5 c,   6 g,   7 a,   8 e
1 predominant in,   2 proportional to,   3 confined to,
4 compatible with,   5 optimum (no dependent preposition),   6 monotonous (no dependent preposition),   7 hostile to,   8 immune to

Exercise 3
1 predominant,   2 proportional,   3 monotonous,
4 compatible,   5 immune,   6 optimum

Exercise 4
1 prompted,   2 incentive,   3 stems,
4 pinpoint,   5 coincided

Part 2:   Practice exercises

Exercise 1
Suggested answers:
1 <u>Where</u> was <u>John born</u>?
2 <u>Why</u> does he <u>love</u> going to the gym?
3 <u>What time</u> does he usually <u>arrive</u> at the <u>gym</u>?
4 <u>How often</u> does he <u>go</u> to the <u>gym</u>?
5 What <u>unusual thing</u> happened to him on his <u>last visit</u>?

Exercise 2
Possible answers:
1 Where is John's place of birth? /
   Where does John come from?
2 What reason does he give for his love of the gym?
3 What time does he normally get to the gym?
4 How many times a week does he exercise?
5 What strange/odd incident did he experience the last time he went?

The order would probably be: b, d, e, c, a.

Exercise 3
1 not answered
2 It gives him energy.
3 5.30 a.m.
4 not answered
5 There was a fire alarm and the sprinklers went off.

Exercise 4
Purpose of the diagram: b (all the labels indicate the parts)
Flow: c
Type of answer:
Question 1: an adjective

Question 2: an adjective (If you look at the other labels, you will see that they are all adjective + noun. In questions 1 and 2, the noun is given, so the answer will very likely be an adjective.)
Question 3: a noun/an adjective (For question 3 the answer will very likely be an adjective + noun combination to follow the other labels. Note that no labels have articles (a/an/the), so you do not need to use them.)

Exercise 5
1 digital, 2 durable, 3 side supports

Exercise 6
1 g, 2 d (This is different from the exact age, e.g. 27. An age group is a range of ages e.g. 21–30), 3 h, 4 f, 5 a, 6 c, 7 e, 8 b

Exercise 7
1 none, 2 swimming ('swim' would be incorrect grammatically), 3 (improve) fitness
Note: she stopped playing tennis so it is not an answer for 2.

Exercise 8
1 b, 3 e, 4 d, 5 c, 6 a, 8 f
Suggested answers:
1 twice a week
3 9.30.
4 Tom, Barbara, Jenny
5 yoga, aerobics
6 Wednesday
8 staff evening off

Exercise 9
1 dance, kickboxing, 2 too hard, 3 (a) conference

Part 3:   Exam practice

Questions 1–3
1 0498355521, 2 silver (membership), 3 11/11th

Questions 4–7
4 club lane, 5 school groups, 6 free swimming, 7 toddlers' pool/toddlers pool

Question 8
8 evenings, Sundays

Questions 9–10
9 (the) television / TV advert, 10 (reach) optimum fitness

10   At the office

Part 1:   Vocabulary

Exercise 1
1 revenue, 2 thrive, 3 commission, 4 collaborate,
5 franchise, 6 restructure, 7 audit, 8 subsidiary

Exercise 2
a thrive, b restructure, c revenue, d collaborate,
e commission, f subsidiary, g audit, h franchise

Exercise 3
1 e, 2 c, 3 h, 4 a, 5 g, 6 b, 7 d, 8 f

Exercise 4
1 collaborate/interact/cooperate,
2 optimises/maximises, 3 revenue,
4 restructure, 5 resolve/settle

Exercise 5
1 A **takeover** is the act of gaining control of a company by buying more of its shares than anyone else. A **merger** is the joining together of two separate companies or organisations so that they become one.
2 The **turnover** of a company is the value of the goods or services sold during a particular period of time. A **profit** is an amount of money that you gain when you are paid more for something than it cost you to make, get, or do it.
3 The **gross profit** is the total amount of profit before any money has been taken away (e.g. through taxes). The **net profit** is the profit which remains when everything that should be subtracted from it (e.g. taxes) has been subtracted.
4 If someone has **copyright** on a piece of writing or music, it is illegal to reproduce or perform it without their permission. A **trademark** is a name or symbol that a company uses on its products and that cannot legally be used by another company.
5 **Marketing** is the organisation of the sale of a product, for example, deciding on its price, the areas it should be supplied to, and how it should be advertised. **Advertising** is the activity of creating advertisements and making sure people see them.
6 People or organisations that **go bankrupt** do not have enough money to pay their debts. If you are **made redundant**, your employer tells you to leave because your job is no longer necessary or because your employer cannot afford to keep paying you.

Exercise 6
1 e, 2 g, 3 b, 4 f, 5 d, 6 h, 7 a, 8 c

Exercise 7
1 entrepreneurs, 2 founders, 3 employees,
4 auditor(s), 5 manager, 6 assistant

Exercise 8
1 c, 2 f, 3 d, 4 e, 5 a, 6 g, 7 h, 8 b

Exercise 9
1 close a deal, 2 signing contracts,
3 raise a point, 4 send (them) an email, 5 minutes the/your meeting

Part 2: Practice exercises

Exercise 1
1 Working in a hotel is more interesting than working in a bank.
2 Both managers and staff in the catering industry earn low salaries.
3 Only a few of the company's employees have (any/some/a lot of) experience in IT.
4 The staff kitchen isn't often clean.
5 The meeting wasn't managed well.

Exercise 2
1 Their finances are audited by an outside accounting company.
2 The travel industry involves working long hours although it sounds glamorous. / The travel industry sounds glamorous although it involves working long hours.
3 Designing modern office buildings is a task which is challenging.
4 Employees were warned about impending job losses by their managers.

Exercise 3
1 a, 2 b, 3 a, 4 a, 5 a, 6 b

Exercise 4
1 assistant, 2 ranges, 3 (client) support

Exercise 5
Suggested answers:
a is activated: sounds/goes off/starts
b make their way to: go to/head in the direction of/walk to/proceed to
c Once outside: When (you are) out of/ After leaving/After exiting
d direct them: show them to/give them directions to/point them towards
e who is responsible for: who is in charge of
f left: gone out of/vacated/made their way out of/exited
g safe to return: all right to go back/no longer dangerous to return/safe to re-enter/not dangerous to go inside

Exercise 6
1 a test, 2 personal belongings,
3 fire marshals, 4 missing people

Exercise 7
Suggested answers:
2 Which person, Sarah, Brian or Helen, makes the reservations for meeting rooms?
3 Which person, Sarah, Brian or Helen, sends weekly email updates to all staff in the company?
4 Which person, Sarah, Brian or Helen, liaises with the cleaning staff?

Exercise 8
Suggested answers:
1 Which advertising medium, newspapers, television, or the internet, will the company be using to advertise children's toys?
2 Which advertising medium, newspapers, television or the internet, will the company be using to advertise baby clothes?
3 Which advertising medium, newspapers, television or the internet, will the company be using to advertise maternity clothes?
4 Which advertising medium, newspapers television or the internet, will the company be using to advertise baby food?
Answers:
1 A, 2 A, 3 C, 4 B

Part 3: Exam practice

Questions 1–3
1 consultancy system, 2 $5,000,000/five million dollars/$5 million, 3 headquarters

Questions 4–6
4 C, 5 B, 6 A

Questions 7–10
7 subsidiary, 8 employees, 9 10%/10 per cent/ ten per cent/ten percent, 10 relocation package

11   Local languages

Part 1:   Vocabulary

Exercise 1
1 b, 2 g, 3 e, 4 i, 5 h, 6 a, 7 d, 8 j, 9 c, 10 f

Exercise 2
1 c, 2 b, 3 f, 4 a, 5 d, 6 e

Exercise 3
1 dialect, 2 sign language, 3 Rhetoric,
4 connotations, 5 transcription, 6 bilingual

Exercise 4
Angela: I thought the lecture on UK regional accents had some credible points about the ways in which English is changing.
Kevin: To be honest, I'm a little bit sceptical of some of the evidence. It seemed to me that their predictions were insufficiently detailed.
Angela: Really? I thought the research methodology appeared to be logical. Maybe the researchers were just cautious with their predictions for the future of English.
1 No
2 Positive: Angela,   Negative: Kevin

3 Angela: credible, logical, cautious (They are positive
and show Angela thought the lecture was good.)
Kevin: sceptical, insufficiently (They are negative
and show that Kevin disagrees with Angela.)

Exercise 5
1 P, 2 N, 3 P, 4 P, 5 N, 6 P, 7 N, 8 P, 9 N, 10 P

Part 2: Practice exercises

Exercise 1
1 (Many) of the (dialects) in the (world) are (gradually
dying out.)
2 Can you (recommend ways) in (which I)
can (improve) my (listening skills?)
3 I'm (researching minority languages)
for my (essay) so (I went) to the (British
library) to (find out more information.)

Exercise 2
1 It sounds more natural the second time.
2 There are many South American Indian
languages, none of which are related to Spanish.
3 Studying accents is a good way to
understand if a language is changing or not.

Exercise 3
1 stopped taking Greek lessons soon after I left school.
2 How will local languages stay in use
if fewer people learn them?

Exercise 4
1 It shows the percentage.
2 None – Welsh, Gaelic, Cornish and Irish are all
languages.
3 It refers to the recent past.
4 a iv, b iii, c i, d ii

Exercise 5
B

Exercise 6
1 c, 2 e, 3 d, 4 a, 5 f, 6 b

Exercise 7
1 central, 2 dialect, 3 language, 4 official, 5 quickly

Exercise 8
1 c, 2 d, 3 b, 4 e, 5 a

Exercise 9
b, d

Part 3: Exam practice

Questions 1–2
1 A, 2 C

Questions 3–6
(In any order) A, B, D, F

Questions 7–10
7 reservation,   8 (local) education authority/
department,   9 the managing director,
10 take photos of

12   Practice test

Section 1

Questions 1–3
1 C,   2 B,   3 B

Questions 4–7
4 14 Brightwell Avenue,   5 032217774,
6 (early) morning,   7 32.25

Questions 8–10
8 (the) changing rooms,   9 (the) shoe
department,   10 (the) cash desk

Section 2

Questions 11–13
11 Midday,   12 (The) shopping district,
13 (The) Military Museum

Questions 14–17
14 C,   15 A,   16 C,   17 B

Questions 18–20
18 the driver,   19 7.00/7/seven,   20 discounts

Section 3

Questions 21–23
21 nocturnal,   22 visual aids,   23 narrow down

Questions 24–26
24–26 (in any order): D, E, G

Questions 27–30
27 long strides,   28 doughnut-shaped/
donut-shaped/doughnut shaped/donut
shaped,   29 lower 30 retractable

Section 4

Questions 31–34
31 (temporary) hours,   32 stone,
33 geographical positioning,   34 decorative

Questions 35–37
35 individuals,   36 globalisation,
37 (70/seventy) laboratories

Questions 38–40
38 A,   39 B,   40 E